Software
Verification and Validation
An Engineering and Scientific Approach

Software
Verification and Validation
An Engineering and Scientific Approach

by

Marcus S. Fisher
USA

 Springer

Marcus S. Fisher
USA
Marcus.S.Fisher@nasa.gov

Software Verification and Validation: An Engineering and Scientific Approach
by Marcus S. Fisher

ISBN 978-1-4419-4100-8

e-ISBN-10: 0-387-47939-2
e-ISBN-13: 978-0-387-47939-2

Printed on acid-free paper.

Printed in the United States of America.

9 8 7 6 5 4 3 2 1

springer.com

Contents

Contents

Preface

The World is lacking an in-depth technical book describing the methods and techniques used to provide confidence in our system software. Not only is the U.S. government more focused on software safety in today's market, but private industry and academia are as well. The methods and techniques that provide such confidence are commonly called *software verification and validation*.

Software Verification and Validation: An Engineering and Scientific Approach, a professional book, fills the critical need for an in-depth technical reference providing the methods and techniques for building and maintaining confidence in many varieties of system software. The intent of this volume is to help develop reliable answers to such critical questions as:

      1) Are we building the right software for the need?
      2) Are we building the software right?

Software Verification and Validation: An Engineering and Scientific Approach is structured for research scientists and practitioners in industry. This book is also suitable as a secondary textbook for advanced-level students in computer science and engineering.

Acknowledgments

As with most work, what starts as a simple idea in the mind of the author leads to a most grueling endeavor for those around him. To those that have been directly affected by this work and have supported me I am thankful. To my parents, Jim and Marsha, for they instilled in me the dedication to see this through and were the first to teach me leadership. To my wife, Hailie, who had to incessantly endure my early morning petulance that resulted from so many late nights on the computer. To her I am grateful for her support, patience, and love during this endeavor. To my future, who has yet to see the light of day but I hope that some day I can give back what has been given to me, opportunities.

Chapter 1: Introduction

Professor Van Lickman desperately calculated his options, he contemplated what could have gone wrong, how could he fix it and how long was it going to take? He knew that he didn't have much time; the launch package was about to cut away the helium balloon that was to carry it to an altitude of 100,000 feet. This was the triggering mechanism for igniting the engines of the model rocket on board the launch package. The rocket was the second stage for this mission that was to prove that off the shelf technology could be used to achieve a low Earth orbit (LEO). Once in orbit, the rocket would autonomously assemble various pieces of hardware that were launched using the same approach. Final assembly would yield a fully assembled spacecraft in LEO that would conduct atmospheric studies of the Earth. The approach had never been tried; recent studies had revealed that fluctuations in Earth's gravity could allow for common technologies to escape the pull of the Earth. That was not on the professor's mind right now, he needed to understand why the vehicle was about to prematurely cut away the helium balloon prior to achieving 100,000 feet. What could have gone wrong?

The Team in the control center worked feverishly, telemetry from the launch package indicated that it was ascending at a rate of 1,000 feet per minute and it was at an altitude of 96,000 feet. The mission was going well up until the last telemetry reading, which showed that the launch package's altitude was 95,990 feet and the onboard computer was about to execute the stored commanding sequence for premature descent. Was the altitude reading wrong or was it accurate? It would take another minute before the next sequence of data was to be sent to the control center and the computer would have executed the abort sequence by then. Without taking action soon, the computer was going to abort the mission. If the professor interrupted the abort sequence and the launch package was descending, it could create a small crater in the Earth at that rate or worse if it was to impact an occupied house. For a premature descent the computer was to cutaway the helium-filled balloon and deploy the rescue parachute in order to slow the rate of descent.

In the end, the professor did not interrupt the abort sequence, the balloon's rate of descent was slowed by the safety parachute and the vehicle was recovered. No one was injured except for the professor's reputation as well as his bank account. The funding entity for his studies lost confidence in the professor and decided not to fund any more experiments. After recovering the launch package and studying all the stored data, pictures from the onboard camera showed that the helium balloon did not fail. How can the balloon still provide lift in the presence of altitude readings indicating the launch package was descending? The professor learned that the last telemetry reading was accurate; the balloon had experienced something that for a brief period of time lowered the altitude by 10 feet. It seemed possible that if there were winds at that altitude they could put the balloon on a horizontal trajectory resulting in the altitude not increasing. If there was a pressure differential at that point in the flight path the launch package could have experienced a momentary drop in altitude. What troubled the professor was that he performed a trade study regarding the ascent rate and how the launch package was to verify it was actually descending. He concluded that he wanted the software to take an altitude reading every minute and if it was less than the last reading then it was to verify on the next reading that it was actually descending. He felt he had accounted for this phenomenon. After careful examination of the software he found that the source code's conditional statement used the assignment operator instead of the equality operator to check for successive readings. As a result no matter what the second altitude reading was, the computer was going to abort the mission. A simple coding error caused him and his team to abort a perfectly good mission.

This is not the desired outcome when operating critical system software. Software that deviates from its expected behavior is not an option when it comes to building safety-critical system software. As such, the professor needed to intelligently employ state-of-the-art tools and methods for assuring his system would not fail during flight. "Of course you have to" you say, every engineer needs to assure that their system will not fail. However, there are various approaches and levels of assurance one can employ and achieve respectively.

System software, like the professors', is an entity that can be observed and studied throughout its entire life, much like biological organisms or natural phenomenon. I'm not just talking about a software system that is deployed and running. Even as the system is being developed, one can study and observe it. But why on Earth would we want to study and observe a software system. Is it something magical or is it going to give us some deeper explanation for the Universe, or is it going to explain the one true use of the googolplex? Let's just simplify matters and ask "How do you know that the software system is going to do what you had intended it to do?" Test it you say, that is certainly part of the answer but I will argue that it is not a complete answer. How do you know that you have tested it under the conditions in which it will experience during operations? By the way I'm not suggesting that I have the silver bullet but I am suggesting that we have a solution that compliments the engineering activities that are performed during development.

To achieve the necessary levels of assurance, engineers have a few options. One of these options is that they can run, in parallel with development, a Verification and Validation (V&V) project. V&V is an engineering practice that provides confidence that the system software was built adequately and will meet the needs of the system. A commonly used definition for V&V is that it is a systems engineering practice that employs methods such as reviews, static and dynamic analysis, testing and formal methods to provide assurance that software artifacts within a certain phase of their life-cycle conform to their requirements and expected operational behavior.

In this book I present a concept that deviates slightly from the commonly used definition. I guess you could say I add a dimension to the V&V concept. In the commonly used definition we state "...provide assurance that software artifacts **within a certain phase** of their life-cycle conform to their requirements and expected operational behavior." I introduce the concept for a systems focused V&V effort. The systems approach goes beyond the individual phases of the life-cycle. It encapsulates the results from all of the phases to make concluding remarks about the system, not just its individual phases. It suggests that V&V is not complete until it integrates the results that conclude each phase. The integrated conclusion represents the system as a whole, not a conclusion for each separate phase of the development life-cycle. For the professor, it wasn't enough to do just the trade study. His concern needed to be followed through each life-cycle phase (i.e. verified the code did what he wanted it to do).

A software system evolves through a process that we traditionally call a life-cycle. It begins with a definition that describes what behavior it is suppose to have. A solution is then created that is supposed to reflect that behavior. This solution is then built and tested against the initial behavioral description. If it passes then it gets deployed, if it doesn't then it gets reworked until it does pass. Artifacts are the byproduct of this evolution. These artifacts represent the system at particular stages of its life. Requirements represent the behavior, designs represent the solution, source code represents the implementation, and tests represent the qualifying argument for deployment.

V&V is itself a process and has a life-cycle of its own. The V&V life-cycle is ran in parallel with the developers. For example, as the behavior

is defined and its byproduct generated (e.g. requirements specification)
V&V will perform requirements analysis. Based on their assessment V&V
will gain an understanding of the system's behavior, will generate specific
facts regarding the quality of the requirements, and may generate issues
with the documented requirements. Figure 1.1 depicts the life-cycle that
V&V traditionally follows. The figure shows the relationships with the
software engineering life-cycle.

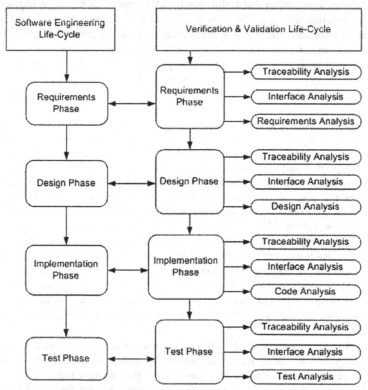

Fig. 1.1. Traditional life-cycle that a verification and validation (V&V) project
will follow. During development, the software evolves through a life-cycle and
the V&V project is ran in parallel.

During the life-cycle V&V conducts focused assessments to assure the
right behavior is being built into the system. For example, the V&V team
performs traceability analysis, interface analysis, and requirements analysis while the development team documents the software requirements.

These analyses are complimentary to the developers. V&V can develop an executable model of the software requirements to be used for their assessments. This additional level of rigor allows the V&V team to assess the requirements from different perspectives than the developers. Development is very focused on engineering the system and proving the system works where V&V explores the various combinations of behavior to show where the system fails. These techniques are what reveal missing functionality or functionality that does not meet the needs of the end user. It is extremely important to discover issues such as these early on in the lifecycle.

Any member of a V&V team or any stakeholder to a V&V project can benefit from this book. They will be able to use this book as a guide when planning, studying or implementing any engineering activity that involves assuring the software behaves as intended. This is not to be taken lightly, a lot of times these practices are overlooked or administered at too high a level to provide any benefit. This book intends to remedy that. This book intends to provide the technical approaches for managers and practitioners so that they not only gain the necessary understanding; they have the detailed steps necessary to achieve their challenging assignments.

There is no cookie-cutter approach for validating that a software system will not fail when orbiting the Earth. However, I lay the framework from which you can begin. I suggest that there are fifteen system-level V&V requirements that must be fulfilled by every V&V effort. It is not a cookie-cutter so to speak simply because the approaches that can be taken to fulfill these requirements can vary. This book introduces the common approaches as well as the objectives that are achieved when performing V&V on system software.

I also want to add that this book is not intended to be a one stop shop for V&V tools. There are too many tools and methods that exist for me to summarize each one of them. I even think that I shouldn't do that. Come tomorrow morning there will be another tool on the market or another tool in the research lab that claims its superiority. So what do I do in this book if I don't present the specific tools? The intent is to provide a baseline for everyone performing V&V. To date there has not been a clear description of what V&V actually achieves when they work on a software project. Most descriptions use terms such as correctness, completeness, and readability without clearly explaining what these terms mean. I want to clear that up. I also want to provide a framework that enables future work to explore and advance the methods and approaches one can take in performing V&V.

The baseline that I wish to establish is to define exactly what V&V has to achieve as well as the level of rigor needed to be realized in their results.

In Chapter 2 I present the management approaches and in Chapter 3 I present the life-cycle that V&V normally follows. Here is where I present the level of rigor as well as the specifics regarding what it is V&V achieves. Chapter 4 is the concluding chapter that summarizes the key topics in the book as well as the concept for systems V&V.

Basically there will be three types of responses to the concepts I introduce within. Some will totally ignore them and think that I've lost my mind. Some will be intrigued by the concepts but will forget about them when they close the book. Others will digest the concepts and in some fashion try to make some or all of them reality. I am trying to reach the latter group of people. I bring this up because these concepts are something that I strongly believe in and I have seen them work in practice. One of the underlying problems that exist is that there are numerous meanings to what V&V is. This is one of the reasons why I wrote this book, I believe that we need to first agree on the core principles and then we can evolve from there. My ultimate goal is to have something that benefits the verification and validation of system software; I am not looking to just develop pages that will later sit on the shelves in my library.

Read these chapters, take notes, and challenge the very ideas that I present. We can not advance anything without challenging the concepts at hand. Concepts that I believe are in their infancy state of scientific structure. Together we can build a theoretical concept for what it truly means to verify and validate a software system.

Chapter 2: Managing Verification and Validation

Even though this book is focused on conveying information to engineers and scientists, I have to include a chapter on management. I have learned from my experiences that the project can not experience success unless management and subject matter experts (SMEs) work together. Numerous times I have fielded questions from the engineers in the trenches like "Why in the world does management want to know that?" It would be much simpler if management only communicated better. It would be just as simple if the engineers in the field fully understood and appreciated exactly what it took to lead a project in its entirety. The data that management uses to develop plans and control the project comes from the SMEs, as such they should fully understand or at least have an idea as to how that data is going to be used. That is why I have included a chapter on management.

A successful Verification and Validation (V&V) project can not be realized unless you have a solid management approach. One aspect of management that first needs to be discussed is leadership. It is essential that you have within your group a few solid leaders with disjoint responsibilities. Your leaders may be your management or may be the junior engineer sitting in the cubicle next to you. Nonetheless, you must be able to recognize her or recognize that it is you and ensure the leadership axioms discussed in the next section are adequately followed on your project. With these axioms comes success, without them comes failure and we all know that failure is not an option.

Leadership is not the only management approach needed for a successful V&V project. This chapter first discusses leadership and the axioms that must be followed if you want to be a successful leader. Section 2.2 discusses the planning approaches that are used to plan a V&V project. This includes establishing the V&V requirements, the scope of the system to be verified and validated, and developing the plan. Section 2.3 discusses managing the project according to the established plan. A complete set of techniques is not introduced simply because this text is not solely about management. Instead I chose to introduce just a few management techniques that I feel must be used and followed to assure the project meets its expectations within +10% and -5% of the established plans. Section 2.4 discusses risk management and section 2.5 introduces the three types of organizational models that a V&V team can employ.

Section 2.1 The Axioms of Leadership

It occurred to me one day while I was attending a design review for a mission that was to travel to low Earth orbit and study the chemical makeup of the Earth's atmosphere, that the people running the review, and held formal titles, were not the actual leaders of the review or of the design team. Granted, I was a naïve young scientist at the time that thought entitlement (e.g. management) brought you control of the engineering of a system. Man was I misled! The Systems Engineer for the mission was clearly the leader. He commanded a certain respect from the design team and his opinion was not only sought after by the management team, it was quickly agreed to. It was interesting to watch the individuals in the room change the very opinions that they were so vigorously arguing for, when he spoke up. The beautiful thing about it was that he never commanded anything, literarily. He knew how to listen, understand the problem that was being discussed, process the data that individuals presented, and make an informed decision. After awhile, I became one of those individuals that looked at him as the leader. From that point forward, I cautiously observed the dynamics of engineering teams in an attempt to figure out, if you don't have the formal title, how can you control everything that goes on? The biggest thing I have learned is that you should not learn how to control; you should learn how to influence!

The objective for this section is to introduce, what I have learned and have practiced myself, the structure, as well as the concepts that all leaders must be familiar with and follow. Leading a group of individuals can be the most complicated engineering task known to humans. However, the foundation for leading is quite simple. Here are the five axioms that you, as a leader, must practice:

- Establish and maintain the problem your team must solve.
- Establish and maintain your environment and organizational structure.
- Establish and maintain how and when your team needs to solve the problem.
- Know your team as you know thyself.
- Establish and maintain a consistent strategy for communication.

Establish and maintain the problem your team must solve

A clearly stated problem that is unambiguous to everyone will produce realistic plans that all team members understand and can follow. The remaining chapters will address the specific problems that a V&V team is trying to solve. The point I'm trying to make in this section is that leaders must ensure that the teams understand what the problems are. It sounds simple, how hard is it to state what the problems are? I challenge you to look at past V&V projects, or the project that you are currently on, and point out the problems that the teams are trying to solve. Don't get me wrong, I'm sure you can generate the problems your team is currently off solving. The underlying challenge is to identify the problems that were established and used to **drive** the goals, objectives, plans, and approach taken by your team.

When you think you have spent too much time in clarifying and stating the problem you must solve, then you need to spend some more. This may not be an easy task and may require a significant amount of effort by doing research, conducting interviews, and surveying the market. Effort needs to be expended to assure that all stakeholders and team members[1] understand the overall problem that will be solved when the project has met its objectives and goals.

Let's first consider a counter example to my assertion that the problem must be clearly stated and understood. A team can put a plan in place, implement the plan, and report on their findings easy enough. They may have even been considered successful. However, I imagine that these counter examples never experienced multiple stakeholders, changing environments, or solved a complex problem. First and foremost, I have learned that it is advantageous for all team members to understand why they are doing what it is they are doing and what their work actually means to the greater cause. Having said that, I'm not implying that you need to have philosophical discussions, group hugs, or bring in the softer sciences so that all team members can get a grip on why they exist. What this means is to simply put the work that is about to be performed into context as well as have it drive the team's plans and tasks.

Here is a simple example. Suppose my goal is to be at the Pittsburgh Airport by noon on January 16. Knowing this goal, I establish the following objectives:

---

[1] Some team members may not realize that they are stakeholders. This is one of the challenges that leaders have and that is making the team aware of why the problem is important, why they should care, and how they fit into the overall solution

- To secure reliable transportation on January 16
- To define a reliable path of travel that is responsive to road conditions
- To arrive at my destination one hour before 12:00 P.M. on January 16

After establishing these objectives, I choose to brainstorm and develop the actions that will be needed to achieve these objectives. These actions will also be incorporated in an overall plan to be followed, however, at this time I chose to brainstorm and get a sense for what I may have to implement. My actions are as follows:

- Secure a rental vehicle for January 15 through January 16.
- Fuel and inspect the rental vehicle on January 15.
- Obtain road-side assistance and determine their average response time.
- Determine the shortest path of travel to Pittsburgh Airport.
- Determine the reliable paths of travel to Pittsburgh Airport taking into consideration traffic, road construction, and possible speeds of travel on January 16.
- Develop the path of travel using the shortest path and reliable paths.
- Develop a time schedule taking into consideration the chosen path as well as having to respond to one failure of the vehicle and one deviation from the established path in order to arrive one hour before 12:00 P.M.
- Establish checkpoints along the path of travel that can be used to manage the trip to Pittsburgh Airport.

After identifying these high-level actions, I put a plan in place and execute it. Upon completion and on January 16th I drive to the Pittsburgh airport. The vehicle does not experience any problems and I don't get lost. As such, I arrive at 10:00 A.M. I have met my goal and I am successful. Upon arrival, I realize the reason that I was to arrive at least by 11:00 A.M. was because I was picking up my wife and her parents that were flying in from Washington D.C. and driving them back to our house. She wanted me there early so that I could meet them to help with their luggage and in case the plane was early. Unfortunately, the vehicle that I rented was a sports car and could only hold two people. This forced me to either put her parents back on the plane, not that I was advocating that nor seeded this fault, or rent another vehicle to accommodate the four of us.

Even though this was an extremely simple example and deemed successful (I arrived at 10:00 A.M.), I am still hearing the disappointment from my wife. I am using this simple example to help explain the importance of understanding the problem and toy examples are good candidates for non-technical explanations. First, in understanding the problem I could have realized why I was going to the Pittsburgh Airport. Even though the goal was very clear, it could be argued that it was not complete. By simply understanding why I needed to achieve this goal I could have alleviated the ultimate problem I was faced with. Second, this information could have been used when planning my tasks. In doing so, I would have realized that I needed a vehicle that could accommodate at least four people with luggage. Lastly, even though I claim success, all the stakeholders did not!

The assertions that I am making are that the problem must be clearly understood and stated in order to establish an accurate goal. Also, a clearly understood and stated problem drives the subsequent objectives and tasks that need to be implemented. A clearly understood and stated problem is essential to manage the changes the project is surely going to experience. And lastly, a clearly understood and stated problem helps the team realize when their solution has met the needs of the system and stakeholders.

As stated before, effort needs to be expended up front to understand the problem and it may not be an easy task. As the leader, make sure you obtain the viewpoint of all stakeholders. Ensure you understand their perspective and what it is they think they want your team to solve. The leader must look beyond the individual tasks and solutions and understand these perspectives and needs because these are the people that may use the system, allocate resources, or are simply in charge. Constantly and consistently keep all stakeholders informed of the problem you are solving and maintain its integrity. When recommended changes surface then manage them by clearly stating that changes can occur but we must assess the impact of implementing the change and whether or not it will compromise the original problem definition. Then and only then can you determine how your approach must change.

Let me make a side note at this point since we are talking about dealing with several types of people. You may not be able to obtain concurrence from all individuals. This presents a very unique challenge. If the one differing opinion happens to belong to your boss then do you say she's right and everyone else must be wrong? How do you handle this for the sake of the team? I can only offer up this advice. Recognize situations where you're not going to win. I know the old cliché, "We don't fight the fights we can win, we fight the fights worth fighting". To me, that is a personal objective and not one you should have your team feel the retributions of if you take them down that path. Instead of leading your team in fighting a doomed struggle, lead your team towards challenges they have a chance of achieving. What this means is that when conflicts arise, it is your responsibility to be able to identify how to resolve them. Actually what I really want to say is, to achieve ultimate leadership, you must be able to anticipate these conflicts before they ever present themselves. Don't leave this paragraph thinking that you should stifle engineers on your team simply because they are arguing with the boss and the boss is always right. What this means is, as a leader, you should see this coming and instead of engaging your team into conflict with your boss, attack it at a different angle. That is where strategy comes into play, and if you haven't read the book "The Art of War" by Sun-tzu, then I suggest you put that on your *"to do"* list. "Ultimate excellence lies not in winning every battle but in defeating the enemy without ever fighting."(Minford 2002)

In defining the problem, always make sure there is a realistic problem that is driving your project. Engineers can be creative; they can easily develop a problem definition even in the absence of a real problem. Time and time again I have seen teams that are building capabilities to only experience pushback, resource constraints, and vague objectives. If you find your self leading a team that is not solving a real problem but building a capability, then you better get training in marketing because you are going to have to sell the hell out of your proposed solution, even though your solution is not really solving anything. You will spend the majority of your time searching for places to use your solution and trying to get others to buy-in to it. Simply put, if you find yourself leading a team that is trying to solve a clearly stated problem that the entire organization and stakeholders understand then you have a recipe for success.

So up until now you are fairly confident that you can state clearly what the problem is that you must solve, unfortunately just stating the problem is not enough. A clearly defined problem statement is not enough to guarantee success, it must be useable. To make it useable, I find it efficient to accompany the problem and maybe even characterize it by defining what the V&V team wants to achieve, a goal and objectives. Defining this is essential! Let me say that again, defining what it is you want to achieve is essential. Realistic goals will not only help the team identify potential risks, they are essential for establishing realistic plans and approaches to solving the problems at hand. It shall be very clear, communicated to all stakeholders and above all, stated up front before the project begins. The more precise you can be in identifying the problem, the more your team can focus on the right solution.

A V&V team never wants to perform just analysis on development artifacts. It must achieve something and not something that is stated for the first time after the fact. For example, a V&V project that performs test analysis on the developer's test cases shall not, after the task is complete, say that it performed test analysis on test cases and found x number of issues. BEFORE test analysis is even started, the goals and objectives must be stated, among other things, planned for and managed. How else would you know when the task is complete? I have seen too many projects that perform analysis on artifacts and quit when they have looked at the last element of the artifact. That is not an adequate exit criteria and that is unacceptable. If you are ever presented this scenario, as the leader you need to recognize that your project will never achieve anything. Recognize this risk and mitigate it!

That is not to say that as a discipline, V&V tasks need to have different goals and objectives for different development Projects. What you want to achieve can be the same for similar artifacts and/or tasks. The important thing is that it is stated up-front, plans are put in place to achieve those objectives and leaders get the team on course and towards those ends. How you implement your approach is what may vary. Then and only then can you lead your team to success.

Now that you have led your team towards ensuring they have a clearly stated problem as well as goals and objectives, it's time to start planning. As a leader, one thing you must keep aware of is whether or not your team has planned enough. Keep in mind; it is not possible to plan a completely risk-free project. There are too many unknowns, too many variables and one of the most common errors is the over analysis of information. Waiting for a solution that has no risk is a nice way to avoid doing anything. It takes leadership and engineering judgment to know when to stop planning and when to take action.

Planning is not a task that is scheduled and identified in a Gantt chart as a one time event! You shall not treat planning that merely gets a check in the box once a formal plan gets developed. Planning is continuous; planning is establishing an adequate approach to solving a problem. If you think that your solution will follow a smooth path and will never deviate from the plans established, then you as the leader either need to quit being the leader or you need to do something about it. Your solution will evolve over the life of the project and your team and plans must evolve with it in order to be successful.

As the leader you need to constantly worry about what may or may not happen. I'm sorry to report that even though V&V teams perform this very well against the projects they are assessing, they do it poorly against their own project. Not enough time is spent in identifying what could go wrong. As a V&V discipline we don't do this enough. You can call this risk management or you could just call it planning using "what if scenarios". Whatever you choose to call it, just call it something and do it! Keep in mind, a V&V team is not successful because everything goes as planned, they are successful because they can react and are ready when things go wrong.

Establish and maintain your environment and organizational structure

It is your responsibility to maintain the organizations integrity. The leaders are the only ones that can adversely affect it. Even though every engineer on the V&V team comes to you for guidance, opinion, or just to blow off steam, it is your responsibility to identify when the chain of command is more appropriate. Once that is broken then you will be leading a band of pirates that do not have the thrust and support of the organization. You might be the most liked person on the team because you ignore management but you will lose the power to influence.

Simple discussions to allow team members to blow off steam are excellent, it is even better if the team comes to you for technical advice. When it comes to team members coming to you because they have a problem with a supervisor, another team member or they want to take an action that is surely going to disappoint management then that is when you have to dawn your coaching hat. As an effective leader you need to then coach the team members, teach them how to approach their team members, supervisors or management. Teach them that they have to exercise the chain of command and emphasize that you will help. You will not only help them but you will maintain that very structure that is needed to produce the final system. Whatever the problem, coach your team to take a route often less traveled by them. More than likely they will have to deviate from their engineering attitude and dawn a more appreciative one. Whether it is a request or they want the team to take a new technical direction, coach them in the following ways:

- Have them understand and gain an appreciation for management's point of view.
- Understand what management is concerned about.
- Identify the weaknesses in your team's point of view and prepare strategies to strengthen them (you don't have to have them strengthened by the time you approach management, but you'll be able to show that you have plans in place).
- Build discussion paths that will be used to keep the discussion focused. Don't let tangential discussions lead you to not solving the problem that you originally came to discuss. Building discussion paths lets you anticipate where discussions may go awry.
- Develop your argument or request by integrating management's point of view into it as well as introduce the things that they may be concerned about. It shows that you have thought through your argument and are ready to move on it.

- Build in a few minor problems into your argument or request. Allow management to easily identify them so that they feel they have contributed and it keeps them from getting tangled up in the details in trying to find problems.
- Lastly, approach them professionally. Take all their ideas as serious ones and make it a point to incorporate all suggestions. That can simply mean that you will go off and explore an idea a little more or it means that it can be easily integrated into your request.

Whether your team member is approaching management or other team members, the ideas listed above are applicable. This will not only maintain a strong organization it will indirectly build your team members professionally. Without a doubt they are excellent engineers, but they may lack the charisma needed to influence others. This is where you, as the leader, can be an effective coach.

Your organization and the environment you are working in must not become stagnant. Even though that is a comfortable environment, for only a short period of time, it will lead to total failure. Your environment must be able to accept change and the advancement in technology that is always occurring. That does not mean that your environment must be an embodiment of chaos at all times, it simply means that you must anticipate chaos, you must expect change, and most of all you must establish an environment that can not only function in its presence, it accepts it with open arms.

An effective mechanism to put in place is an advanced technology capability that is focused on an aggressive tools and technologies development process. This process should continually update standard operating procedures, produce new platforms, and extend training into new and diverse areas. To do this may require extra work on your part. But once you do it the first time and have data that supports it take it to management. Together you will discover that a culture that emphasizes the need to aggressively search for and test new solutions effectively and easily allows the projects to respond to changes as well as unforeseen problems.

Establish and maintain how and when your team needs to solve the problem

I have seen V&V teams function time and time again without using knowledge of what worked before. I am guilty of this as well. I have learned that it is essential to incorporate previous successes as well as failures. Domain experts certainly bring this knowledge to the table indirectly, but you take the chance and are gambling that your grey beards will effectively incorporate the best practices of the past.

Essentially what I'm referring to are best practices. As a leader, you must ensure that best practices are documented after tasks are completed. It is not enough to only document these best practices. They must be used! These practices must be employed when formulating plans and approaches and as a leader, you must hold the team accountable for showing that these practices are actually being used.

Using best practices is extremely important to solving your current problem. But best practices alone will not maintain the integrity of the solution. Sometimes engineers and scientists lose focus of the overall goal and objectives. They can be the most creative people I've met and when they get on a problem or a solution it is nearly impossible to change their course. That is why you must keep them focused on solving the problem at hand. They can easily get off on tangential solutions that may be cool, but do nothing in meeting the overall goals and objectives. You can't stifle them by telling them that the problem they are investigating is useless but if the problem they are working on does not lead to a solution to the one established at the beginning of the project then you better get a handle on it.

I once worked with an engineering team and one of our tasks were to verify that all commands from a spacecraft's master command database, was being executed by the developer's test procedures. It was a fairly straightforward problem but it soon developed into an unmanageable one. I was under the impression that the team was off tracking commands and the parameters being passed to each, when during our weekly tag-up I received status that surprised me. The team reported that they had acquired actual operational logs that identified the commands that had been executed by a spacecraft our project was inheriting its' software from. Using the command logs, they were going to develop a graph that depicted which software tasks were spawned as a result of each command being issued. Using that, the team would be able to identify which "pieces" of the software have actually been exercised on orbit. Their logic was to determine which commands had the most impact on the system software and hence which aspects of the system should be exercised more frequently by the test procedures. This had all transpired within one week's worth of time. Needless to say I had two major comments. First, I thought that would be cool as hell if we could provide that kind of capability and second, I thought I was going to strangle my team of highly qualified engineers. They had totally lost focus of the task at hand. I had to suppress my inner satisfaction for being impressed with their idea in order to get them back on the original problem. However, to do so was a challenge. Never and I mean never, tell an engineer that they shouldn't be doing something, unless it is illegal. What I mean, is that we are explorers by nature and intelligent minds are hard to manage. Instead of telling them to quit what they were doing and that we had no use for it I worked with them by continuously talking about the original problem "verifying that all commands from the spacecraft's master command database, was being executed by the developer's test procedures" and how their solution was going to give that to us in the time-frame identified. Even though they couldn't answer, they were still elated with the new approach that they had just developed. I had to agree that it was a great approach, but just not for the problem that we were suppose to be solving. I negotiated with them, I got them back on track in solving the original problem and I secured a few extra dollars to do a research project that allowed them to explore their new found ideas.

You could say I caved in and instead I should have commanded them to stop what they were doing and get back on the original task, but then I would have run the risk that their engineering minds would have become stale. In the end, I now take into consideration a few things before I get started on a project. First, when putting plans together I assess each of the tasks and the problem being solved. Things that I'm looking for are ways those eager engineering minds might stray from the objectives during implementation. I use this information to help me decide the type of communication that is needed within the team. I may use a weekly meeting that all team members must attend, instead of just the leads. This allows me to get a good feel for what is actually going on in the project instead of hearing it second hand. Another very effective technique is to institutionalize an environment that accepts all new ideas and supports them. Advocate to the team that we seek to do things that are innovative but we must manage the risk that is inherent with innovation. Keep focused on the original problem but let the team know that they can come to you with new ideas for doing things and there is a possibility for implementing new approaches. This maintains their explorative nature as well as it keeps you informed where the team may be straying.

Know your team as you know thyself

Practitioners of V&V need to first learn by doing, we must be equally knowledgeable as the designers of the system that we are performing V&V on. If you are leading a V&V team that has not experienced the dynamics of engineering a system or can not appreciate and understand what it takes to build a system, then you have no chance of succeeding. Having a team that is technically competent is one thing, maintaining that technical competency is another. Institutionalize a rigorous training program that allows

your team to constantly stay abreast of the engineering advancements going on around them and advocate a mentality that we are the "Best of the
best!"

A slogan like "Best of the best!" is useless if it is simply printed to a
plaque and mounted to a wall to collect dust. You have to lead your team
from in front, put yourself on the frontline and show them the type of behaviors that are characteristic for being the best. To do this means you
must also be as knowledgeable as your team, you must be an expert in the
discipline. This will gain their respect and will better enable you to effectively lead and make informed decisions. Does this mean you have to
know everything, of course not! Enforce customized leadership. You may
not be the appropriate leader in all situations. But you should be able to
recognize who is. Then you should not only step aside but somehow get
that person to step up as the leader. This is putting leadership theory into
practice. Recognize who the experts are and who you should be seeking
knowledge from, make it public to show that you are not only a team
player, but you recognize the contribution of others. This is easily done if
you know your team members, know what they do but know the difference
between knowing your team members' jobs and doing it for them. Don't
micromanage, trust the team and communicate that you do.

Micromanaging or testing your team's actions breeds distrust and in an
environment that has increasingly become a world of individuals only hin-
ders your chances of building an effective team. Competition among the
team has increased, which can be good but it can also be bad. You must
emphasize and encourage the concept that even though individual successes are good, team work is more important. The minute you start questioning individual team members' work the more they will become defen-
sive. Give authority to your team members so that they can accomplish
the tasks, advocate responsibility and above all, make the team accountable. Promote relationships amongst the team and above all, back your
people up. Your team members can disagree with each other and you can
disagree with them, just don't do it out in public. Back-up your team's actions at all times and if it was wrong, take care of it off-line, never do it
outside of the team.

Establish and maintain a consistent strategy for communication

The biggest mistake in the world that a leader can make is to not communicate to the team regarding what is going on. Sealing oneself off and
concealing the reasoning behind decisions will quickly make a once cohe-
sive team become a gang of mercenaries. It is very simple and I have no
idea why it gets screwed up time and time again. Establish a routine

mechanism to get the word out. I advocate that a standing meeting that occurs at a frequency appropriate for the project is advantageous to all team members. Whether it is a daily meeting or weekly meeting, you must have face-to-face meetings with your team. Scheduling and conducting the meeting is the first step, you still have to make it structured and effective by establishing goals and objectives for the meeting.

Only make it a required meeting for those that can benefit from attending. Communicate why each of the participants is involved. It is not so that they can show mastery of the details in their area of responsibility. But to receive and share information that would be useful to the entire team. Lastly, make it clear that all participants are welcome to speak, but it is not required. As we all have experienced, some people like to talk just to hear their own voice. Make it clear that this will not be tolerated.

Keep the meeting focused on the objectives. Don't let discussions deviate too far from the main discussion points and don't waste the participant's time. Let them know that someone is in charge by stopping those tangential discussions and refocus the group. And above all, make a damn decision during the meeting. Don't let topics go on and on and suggest a follow-up meeting to solve it (unless there is no way around it).

The meeting is a chance for your team members to communicate their ideas in an orderly way. All new ideas should be brought to the meeting. It is not a good idea to let team members skirt the meeting and pitch their ideas to you directly. They need to be brought in front of the team. Other team members have valuable information that could contribute and enhance the suggestions.

Meetings can serve several purposes like decision making, communication, and networking. Networking in the sense that it allows the team members to get together and socialize. You don't need to hold a mixer but it is good to let them socialize among the team. Hold yourself accountable as well as others and show them that you will. To promote open and effective communication, you need to communicate to the team that encountering problems is expected but failing to mention problems or even worse, covering them up, is not tolerated.

Meetings can be very effective but you must establish goals and objectives, let the participants know why they are required to be there, keep the meeting focused on the objectives, establish a structured forum to communicate new ideas, and allow the team to socialize among themselves. If these ideas are followed, then you will quickly realize the advantages for holding them. If you don't adhere to these basic principles then it will become just another meeting to waste time.

The objective for this section was to introduce some structure, as well as the concepts, that all leaders must be familiar with and follow. Are these axioms an exhaustive set for which all great Leaders will emerge? I encourage all readers to put forth some extensive thought on these assertions and I challenge you to come up with additional axioms or even question those presented here. To put into practice and challenge these axioms would in fact help you rise above that which I can only convey. This would be a true display of leadership and possibly the creation of another axiom "lead others to become better leaders than you."

Section 2.2 Planning

Planning the V&V effort is a reoccurring task used to assure V&V resources are efficiently identified and allocated. Planning also establishes the goals and objectives for the V&V effort. I must emphasize that it is a reoccurring task and not merely performed at the beginning of the project to never be addressed again. Management, scientists, and engineers must work together through the course of the project to assure that realistic plans are established and maintained. It is not possible to plan a completely risk-free project. There are too many unknowns and too many variables to consider. As such, plans need to be reassessed during the life of the project.

Planning can be organized into a series of steps. These steps are identified in Table 2.1.

Table 2.1. Process Steps for Planning V&V.

Planning Process Step	Description
Establish V&V mission	Develop the goal for the V&V project.
Identify V&V stakeholders	Identify those entities that have a vested interest in the V&V project.
Identify V&V stakeholder requirements	Identify the needs and expectations of the stakeholders.
Establish the V&V objectives	Identify five to seven results that define a successful V&V project.
Develop a concept	Develop a high-level approach depicting how the V&V project will operate.
Develop V&V requirements	Using the stakeholder requirements, V&V concept, and the standard V&V requirements develop the system requirements for the V&V project.
Establish V&V scope	Using the V&V objectives, identify the software components that will be assessed during the project.

Develop a Work Breakdown Structure (WBS)	Identify the products that will result from the V&V effort and the tasks responsible for developing the products.
Develop network diagram	Using the work packages from the WBS, develop the temporal relationships between work packages.
Estimate resources	Using a bottoms up approach, estimate the budget using the work packages.
Develop project plan	Using the results of the previous steps, develop the project plan.

The following sections discuss the concepts that make up each of the steps in Table 2.1. Section 2.2.1 presents an approach to establishing the V&V requirements, which includes identifying stakeholder requirements, establishing objectives, developing the V&V concept, and establishing the V&V scope. Section 2.2.2 presents the development of the V&V plan. I only present an overview regarding the work breakdown structure (WBS), network diagram, and resource estimation because this book is not solely focused on management approaches. These concepts are basic in nature and well defined in numerous management books.

Section 2.2.1 Establishing the V&V Requirements

The backbone with any project is the technical scope of the work to be performed, or the requirements. It can make and break projects. Let me reiterate, the technical scope of the work can make or break projects. Not only must you assure that the appropriate scope is established, you must manage that scope such that the established goals and objectives can be met. Managing the technical scope of the work is discussed in section 2.3; this section discusses establishing the scope of work.

Common knowledge, as well as practice has demanded a rigorous approach towards developing the requirements for a project. At least 10 – 15% of the project's budget should be used for the up front planning, which includes defining the requirements.

The purpose for this up front planning is to establish the V&V requirements as well as the software systems that fall within scope of the V&V effort. There are two approaches that can be taken to plan a V&V project. The first approach is a systems engineering approach that is being introduced for the first time and is described in section 2.2.1.1. The second approach is the one defined in the IEEE Standard 1012 and is presented in section 2.2.1.2 for reasons of being complete.

Some discussion is warranted as to the reason for the two approaches. The approach outlined in the IEEE standard is based on the fact that the V&V project cannot perform every possible analysis task known to the engineering community. As such, a decision-making methodology is needed to identify which V&V tasks are needed to be performed based on the criticality of the software. Several factors are taken into consideration when determining the criticality of the software (e.g. impact to system performance if the software fails). I am not opposed to this approach and it can be very useful. The reason for me to develop the systems engineering approach is to lessen the subjectivity and make the planning effort more requirements driven. This is my attempt to evolve the practice of V&V towards a systems engineering discipline. This is discussed more in the appropriate sections.

Section 2.2.1.1 Systems Engineering Approach

The planning approach outlined in this section is being introduced for the first time and will surely receive an enormous amount of scrutiny. To this I reply, excellent! My attempt is to evolve the practice of V&V into a systems engineering discipline, one that is not perceived as being ad hoc and vague. The objectives for the systems engineering approach is twofold, first I want the approach to clearly identify what can be expected to be achieved once V&V has completed and secondly, I want the approach to clearly identify why V&V is doing what it is doing (i.e. why do test analysis on my software development project). This approach follows the steps outlined in Table 2.1.

The systems engineering approach differs from the approach outlined in the next section in two ways:

- It uses the same approach as an engineer would use if they had to develop a system.
- It does not involve the selection of which tasks need to be performed.

I submit to you that using the same approach as you would if you had to engineer a system is advantageous for several reasons. First, it is nothing new, all engineers understand the approach taken to develop a system (e.g. define objectives, develop requirements). Secondly, it is requirements driven. It starts with defining WHAT the V&V project shall achieve and the characteristics they must have. Instead of defining how the V&V team is going to function (e.g. perform traceability analysis) it focuses on defining what the required capabilities need to be (e.g. provide assurance that the software will reliably recognize system faults and respond adequately).

The other major difference is that this approach does not go through the process of selecting which tasks the V&V team shall perform. As you'll see in the next section, a criticality approach performs certain V&V tasks based on the criticality of the software. The systems approach semantically diverges in order to provide some organization and unification to V&V. The systems approach traverses all the phases in the V&V life cycle (e.g. traceability analysis, interface analysis, requirements analysis, design analysis, code analysis and test analysis). Actually what I'm trying to get across is that those "tasks" that I just mentioned are not really tasks, they represent the life cycle that a V&V project traverses. The reason is that in order to gain the necessary assurance (if you didn't want assurance then you wouldn't be doing V&V) a complete systems perspective has to be obtained. In addition, for the V&V project to draw conclusions about the software, the entire system needs to be assessed. The entire system in this case includes the requirements, designs, code, and tests. This means that the entire life cycle has to be exercised in order to provide verification and validation on system software.

The first time one reads these paragraphs they will immediately conclude that taking such an approach is not feasible. The budget alone would not support a V&V project that executes every phase. I have two responses. The first is emotionally based and it is similar to arguing that it is not feasible for the development team to define the requirements of the system. They shouldn't execute the requirements phase! Similarly, arguing that certain engineering tasks should not be performed because of a limited budget. The driving question is not "should they execute the requirements phase", the driving question is HOW should they execute the requirements phase. I submit to you that the V&V team is no different. The development project, if they were budget driven, may elect to write requirements on the back of a bar napkin. No matter how they do it to meet their budget constraints, they are still going to define their requirements. That is the same for V&V. The systems approach requires that V&V perform requirements analysis no matter what, it is not open for discussion. How the V&V team performs the task is how they can make it feasible. They may elect to only review the presentation material at the requirements review over a two week period. They still performed requirements analysis and make an engineering assessment on the requirement's quality but they did it within the constraints of the budget.

The non-emotional response goes something like this, you are correct in assuming that it may be unfeasible to execute every life cycle phase. Again, that is an assumption. What we have to consider before we can conclude with any certainty is HOW those phases shall be implemented in order to meet the V&V objectives. What I'm saying is that even though I am suggesting that requirements analysis is performed by the V&V team every time they work on a project, how they implement that is totally dependent on the objectives that they have to meet. For example, on one project the V&V team may need to bring in tools to statically analyze the requirements in order to meet their objectives. On another project, the V&V team may be comfortable with attending the requirements review in order to meet their objective. These examples would produce two entirely different resource needs. My point that I'm trying to make, it's about time you're probably thinking, is that up front planning needs to focus on WHAT needs to be achieved first and then concentrate on HOW it is going to be implemented. As such, when using the systems engineering approach we do not focus on how we are going to perform the V&V tasks. Instead we focus on defining what the V&V objectives are and plan for how to meet them. The standard set of V&V tasks are simply a life cycle that represents an order of execution. Figure 2.1 depicts this life cycle as well as introduces the four basic approaches to implementing V&V; manual analysis, static analysis, dynamic analysis, and formal analysis. The approaches to implementing V&V are what can vary to meet budget constraints and more importantly to meet the objectives established in the planning phase. These approaches are discussed in greater detail later in this section as well as in Chapter 3.

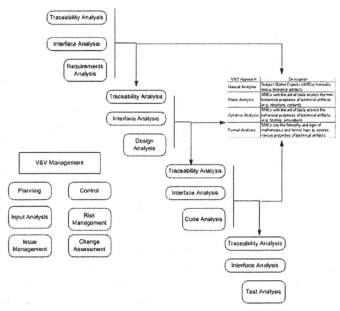

Fig. 2.1. The Verification and Validation Life Cycle. Management tasks are performed throughout the life-cycle. There are four basic approaches that can be taken to implement the V&V tasks within a phase. The approaches are categorized as manual analysis, static analysis, dynamic analysis, and formal analysis.

Defining the objectives is not a simple task. We have learned this from years of engineering systems. However, it is not impossible. The V&V team needs to define measurable objectives that can be used to define what it means for the V&V project to be successful. But how can you do this? First and foremost, the overall goal of the V&V project needs to be identified as well as the stakeholders. Stakeholders are categorized as either active or passive.

Active stakeholders are those entities that have a vested interest in the V&V project and will interact with the V&V project. Interaction could be in the form of using the V&V results to simply communicating with the V&V team.

Passive stakeholders are those entities that have a vested interest in the V&V project and can somehow influence the success of the effort. Influence also comes in many flavors, from standards that affect how the V&V team performs their work to network administrators that influence which tools can be installed on the network.

This is an extremely important step, one that is not to be taken lightly by any means and it is very straight forward. Do not read anymore into it. It is a basic concept; identify those that care about the V&V effort. Even though it may be extremely simple to do, it is often over looked. As a good leader, as you saw in the beginning of this chapter, you have to manage the expectations of those that can possibly influence your results.

Once the stakeholders are identified, you must elicit their requirements or expectations that they may have for the V&V effort. You can hold informal sessions to discuss it, conduct interviews, perform surveys, or research previous V&V efforts. I am not prepared to insert an entire chapter on requirements engineering, that wouldn't even be enough anyway, so I point you to any requirements engineering book regarding this topic. The concepts are quite similar.

As the stakeholder requirements are being gathered the V&V team can begin studying the existing system requirements and operational needs of the system they are to V&V. The intent is to gain a thorough understanding of the operational needs and performance needs of the system. The bottom line is that a combination of the stakeholder requirements, system requirements, and operational needs shall generate the V&V objectives. Figure 2.2 depicts the integration of information that makes up the V&V objectives.

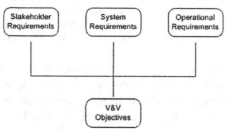

Fig. 2.2. Information Flow for Generating V&V Objectives

Let's take Project MUGSEY 0x01 as an example. MUGSEY is a University project that experiments with using off the shelf technology to reach low Earth orbit (LEO). It is described more in the appendix but basically it is a scientific platform attached to a helium balloon. The V&V team on the project has to first identify the goal of their effort. This is where they identify the need or the problem that the V&V team shall solve.

MUGSEY V&V Goal

The goal of the V&V project is to assure that the software maintains the system's health, acquires and maintains operational data and is adequately developed to efficiently enable future missions.

The goal is very high-level but it is concise; it suggests that the V&V team is going to assure that the software is capable of maintaining the health of the system as well as maintaining the science data that is collected. Clarity is added as the V&V team refines the goal into achievable objectives. That when combined and met shall satisfy the goal.

The second step is to identify the stakeholders, those entities that have a vested interest in the V&V effort. For the V&V effort on MUGSEY 0x01, the following list of stakeholders has been identified.

- MUGSEY 0x01 Management
- MUGSEY 0x01 Developers
- MUGSEY 0x01 Operations Team
- University Scientists
- Society of Gravitational Studies (SOGS)
- University Network Administrators
- University Software Engineering Department

The following list of items depicts the requirements that each stakeholder has for the V&V effort. These requirements are followed by some rationale to further explain the stakeholder's expectation. These requirements do not have to be formal requirements (i.e. written with shall statements) they represent the stakeholder's need or their expectation that they have for the V&V effort. These were acquired by meeting with the stakeholders and discussing their responsibilities and concerns.

MUGSEY 0x01 Management

- I need all the interfaces verified that the observatory segment has with other segments in the system.

Rationale: The project manager anticipates a decoupled architecture that relies on communication between software modules. This will allow different university students to work on different modules of the system. In addition, MUGSEY's architecture is going to leverage a modularized design so that scientists that use MUGSEY can easily integrate and swap out their scientific experiments. To that extent, the project manager wants additional assurance that the interfaces will not cause a problem when they integrate the system.

- I do not want the V&V team to slow down or adversely affect the production of my development team.

Rationale: The project manager has had some bad experiences with previous V&V efforts and does not want the V&V effort to impede development.

- I want all V&V issues resolved with the development team directly.

Rationale: The project manager does not want to waste time on the formality of resolving issues. He wants valid issues that the V&V team identifies to be resolved efficiently. Also, he does not want to create a hostile environment between V&V and development. Developers may get the wrong impression if the V&V team takes all the issues to management.

- I want all V&V results communicated to me directly (monthly status and technical reports for each task).

Rationale: The project manager wants timely feedback on the quality of the system. Also, he wants technical documents that come out of the V&V effort to be entered into the project's artifact repository.

- I need the fault management system on MUGSEY to work flawlessly so that we can recover the system in real time.

Rationale: The project manager has envisioned several failure scenarios and wants, without question, to recover from any fault. His concern is that the balloon may get away from the operations team and possibly fall at a high rate of speed and damage something. As such, they are building a fault management system that maintains awareness of the systems health and responds appropriately.

- I need all the data to be recovered so that collaborating scientists can use it.

Rationale: The project manager stated very bluntly that without the science data then there is no use in funding the mission.

- I need the software to be able to be reused with minimal effort.

Rationale: The project wants to be able to fly again in one week after each mission. Also, each mission may have different science experiments plugged into the observatory. The software has to be easily maintained to make such changes.

- I need the software to be easily understood by other developers so that I can bring on graduate students in the future.

Rationale: The project manager is using university students to develop the system. It will take longer than one semester and it will need to be maintained. As such, different students with varying levels of experience will be employed on the project.

MUGSEY 0x01 Developers
- We need to easily resolve the issues that the V&V team identify.

Rationale: Schedules are tight and the development team consists of graduate engineering students. They actually fear the V&V effort and believe the V&V project will have an adverse affect on their production.

- We need access to the V&V tools and models.

Rationale: The development team needs to be able to not only understand the issues that the V&V team raise but they'll need to reproduce them and verify that they have fixed them. As such, they want access to the tools and models used by the V&V team.

MUGSEY 0x01 Operations Team
- We need to recover all telemetry sent by the launch package. We need to be able to communicate with the launch package any time we need to.

Rationale: The operations team has a very strict requirement levied on them to be able to maintain safe conditions at all times. One of their fears is that the baloon will get away from them and they won't be able to maintain contact.

- We need the mission to be able to avoid hazardous zones.

Rationale: During operations the team is going to infer flying and landing zones of the baloon. Accuracy is needed to assure they avoid hazardous areas.
- We would like to see the V&V results in case operational procedures are needed for work arounds.

Rationale: If any problems or risks are accepted by the project and not fixed the operations team needs to be aware of them so that procedures during flight could be put in place to avoid those issues from surfacing during operations.

University Scientists
- We need to be able to plug our science experiments with minimal difficulty into MUGSEY.

Rationale: Scientists are going to be able to build their experiments separately from the main development team and then just plug their experiments into the observatory segment. They are building their experiments against the interface specification as well as an engineering emulator of the observatory segment. They don't want to find out there are problems when it is too late, meaning they don't want the problems to surface when they try to integrate the experiment.

- We need to be able to extract our science results with minimal difficulty.

Rationale: The scientists work is totally dependent on getting the science data. They need all the data that they capture returned to them.

Society of Gravitational Studies (SOGS)
- The project has to come in on cost and on schedule.

Rationale: This is the funding source for the development project and they are concerned with the management of resources.

- The mission has to recover all the data captured during operations.

Rationale: Not only is the funding source concerned about resources they want a good return on their investment, which tranlates to scientific data.

- The mission needs to do everything possible to avoid harming anyone or damaging any property or other material.

Rationale: They want to protect their image as well as protect individuals and property.

These requirements capture the expectations of those that may interact with the V&V team. These requirements need to be studied and then filtered. Why filtered? Well let's first examine why we even executed this step. Why did we even identify who the stakeholders were and what their needs were? You may even be an independent V&V (IV&V) team that is chartered to do what the V&V team thinks they should do and not be constrained by the stakeholders and as such should not be concerned with their needs. With that I would say that you are foolish. Any good engineer knows that they have to manage the expectations of all entities that are associated with the system. As such, it is beneficial to the V&V team, no matter their organizational structure, to understand what it is that other people are expecting or would like to see come out of the V&V effort. That doesn't mean that you have to do everything the stakeholders need, just understand their needs and use them appropriately. The filtering mechanism is one that is associated with the organizational model the V&V team is assuming. If they are an embedded V&V team then the stakeholder requirements may be written in stone and those are the requirements that the V&V team shall fulfill. If the V&V team is independent then it is advantageous for them to understand what others would like to get out of the V&V effort and they could manage these expectations appropriately.

The stakeholder requirements, the project's system requirements, and the project's operational needs will then be used to develop the objectives for the V&V effort. The V&V team needs to identify five to seven results that define what it means to be successful when complete. Take note that these objectives will later be used to define the scope of the V&V effort. The objectives of the MUGSEY 0x01 V&V effort are to:

- Provide assurance that the system software adequately analyzes and maintains the system's health.
- Provide assurance that the system software adequately identifies and handles faults.
- Provide assurance that the system software adequately acquires, stores, and retains data.
- Provide assurance that the system software can reliably communicate with the ground.
- Provide assurance that the system software is maintainable.

To recap, these objectives are the factors that the V&V team is going to strive to meet. They clearly articulate exactly what the V&V team is going to achieve as they are doing their assessments as well as when they have completed.

Let's just take a moment to assess the systems engineering approach to planning the V&V effort. As stated before, one of the objectives of the systems approach was to clearly identify what can be expected to be achieved once V&V has completed. So far we have identified what the V&V goal is, who the stakeholders are, and developed V&V objectives that encapsulate their needs. Just a note, the objectives do not have to only satisfy the stakeholder's needs. The objectives can also encapsulate other items that V&V feel are of importance. The main point is that everyone remains aware of the objectives. The rationale is simple, the V&V effort is to be planned to not only be able to efficiently allocate resources but to solve applicable problems. To me, this approach clearly shows what V&V will achieve once they have completed. For example, there is no question as to what can be expected from the V&V team. There is an agreed upon objective that clearly shows that the MUGSEY project can expect the V&V team to provide additional assurance that the fault management component of MUGSEY will work reliably. This is only one part of the planning exercise. The second part is to clearly identify why V&V is doing what it is doing.

Once the objectives are defined the V&V team needs to understand what it may look like when they execute their V&V tasks. This can be in the form of a concept of operations. The concept is used to explore the possible approaches that can be taken to interact with the project and meet the V&V objectives. Developing a concept is something extremely beneficial to the V&V team. It lays the foundation for how the team will operate once they begin execution. It is a very valuable planning tool and comes in handy when communicating with the project. As an example, Figure 2.3 is the concept for the MUGSEY 0x01 V&V Project. The top part of the figure depicts how the V&V effort is going to be organized with respect to the developing organization. This just shows the communication paths as well as entities that are involved. You could even add data flows to this diagram so that all parties know the types of information to be generated as well who will receive it. The bottom part of the figure shows an example sequence during the requirements phase between the V&V team, MUGSEY management, and the developers. What I can't stress enough is that this high-level planning tremendously helps everyone understand how they are going to interact during the life of the project. Defining this up front only helps the V&V team during execution.

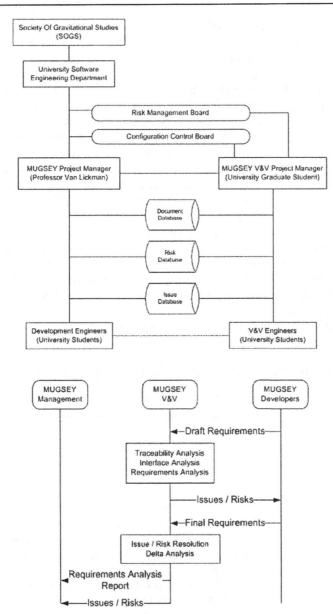

Fig. 2.3. Example concept of operations for the MUGSEY V&V effort

Now that the goal and the objectives have been defined, it is the responsibility of management and subject matter experts to establish the V&V

requirements. The V&V requirements are a culmination of the stakeholder requirements, the V&V concept, and the standard V&V requirements.

Discussion is needed regarding the standard V&V requirements. I had stated earlier that the systems approach to planning requires that every phase of the V&V life cycle is to be executed. This is the result of that statement. I am asserting that there exists a standard set of system requirements that V&V must fulfill every time. Actually there are at least 15 system requirements that V&V must fulfill every time. Meaning, if V&V is working on a system for the Internal Revenue Service (IRS) then they will meet this set of requirements. If they are working on a University system that auctions off textbooks then the V&V team will meet this set of requirements. When a group of engineers perform V&V then they will meet this set of requirements.

It is quite simple; you start with the standard set of system requirements, fifteen in all, and add to the set if they do not cover those identified by the stakeholders or the concept. Usually, the requirements that are added are nonfunctional requirements. Keeping in mind that scope specific statements (e.g. fault management) is not part of the requirements but is part of just that, the scope.

The standard set of system requirements that the V&V team must fulfill are depicted in Table 2.2.

Table 2.2. Standard Set of V&V Requirements. During each phase of the life-cycle the V&V team shall fulfill the requirements within Traceability Analysis, Interface Analysis, and Technical Analysis. How they fulfill these requirements is dependent on the developer's artifacts as well as the approaches the V&V team choose.

V&V Requirement No.	Title	V&V Requirement
3.1	Traceability Analysis	
3.1.1		V&V shall assure all the appropriate parent elements and child elements are in a relationship.
3.1.2		V&V shall assure that the parent elements are related to the right child elements.
3.1.3		V&V shall assure that relationships are consistent in their level of detail.
3.2	Interface Analysis	
3.2.1		V&V shall assure that the right interface elements have been identified.
3.2.2		V&V shall assure all the interface elements are

		completely defined.
3.2.3		V&V shall assure that each interface element is used consistently.
3.2.4		V&V shall assure interface elements maintain the performance needs of the system.
3.2.5		V&V shall assure that interface elements are testable.
3.3	Technical Analysis	
3.3.1		V&V shall assure the right child elements have been identified.
3.3.2		V&V shall assure the child element satisfies the parent element.
3.3.3		V&V shall assure the child elements are completely defined.
3.3.4		V&V shall assure that each child element is used consistently.
3.3.5		V&V shall assure the child element complies with appropriate standards and engineering practices.
3.3.6		V&V shall assure the logic and computational precision satisfy the needs of the system.
3.3.7		V&V shall assure all child elements are testable.

These fifteen system requirements represent the system level requirements that the V&V team shall fulfill. These are the characteristics that precisely show what is needed from the V&V team. The terms parent element and child element are used several times in these system requirements and require some explanation. They will be further defined once these system level requirements are refined but some explanation will be given now. The V&V team performs assessments against artifacts. For example, the V&V team is going to assess the software design of the system. The design of the system represents a solution for the software requirements. For the V&V team to assess the design they will need to assess it against the software requirements. The design, in this case, would be the child element stated in the V&V requirements and the requirements would be the parent element stated in the V&V requirements. So in order for the V&V team to fulfill the technical analysis requirements (See Technical Analysis requirements 3.3 in Table 2.2) for the design, the V&V system level requirements would be refined into V&V subsystem level requirements such as:

- V&V shall assure the right design elements have been identified.
- V&V shall assure the design elements satisfy the requirements.

- V&V shall assure the design elements are completely defined.
- V&V shall assure that each design element is used consistently.
- V&V shall assure the design elements comply with appropriate standards and engineering practices.
- V&V shall assure the logic and computational precision satisfy the needs of the system.
- V&V shall assure the design elements are testable.

This may take some time in getting use to. Picture V&V as being developers. In the development world you would state your requirements and then develop a solution to the requirements. I am proposing that V&V act in a similar fashion. These 15 system requirements represent exactly what the V&V team's assessments shall fulfill. They can be easily used to communicate what is needed from V&V so that they can make a complete assessment against the system they are to verify and validate. Additional requirements can be added if they are not covered by these standard ones. For example, I would add the following non-functional requirements to the MUGSEY 0x01 V&V effort to fulfill the stakeholder's expectations:

- The V&V team shall minimize the amount of effort involved with the resolution of issues.
- The V&V team shall resolve issues with the development team.
- The V&V team shall develop and deliver a monthly status report to the Project Manager.
- The V&V team shall develop and deliver a technical report for each V&V task performed.
- The V&V team shall assure the software is maintainable.

These requirements are then used to architect a solution. Once the V&V team identifies WHAT it is they need then they can identify HOW they are going to meet these requirements. Are they going to test the system, are they going to model the requirements and do dynamic analysis to assure the behavior is what was expected. My point is that now you can start coming up with a solution. To me, the V&V project is not complete if you dive right in and identify how you are going to verify and validate the system. I feel the first thing that needs to be accomplished is defining what it is you want to achieve and be very clear with it by stating it as requirements.

I don't want to discuss the V&V approaches to meeting these requirements as of yet but I'll give an example since this concept is new. For every V&V project they must meet the standard set of V&V requirements. During each phase of the life-cycle you must meet the requirements for traceability analysis, interface analysis, and technical analysis. For example, you will have to come up with a solution for meeting the requirements for traceability analysis. If you are in the implementation phase you will need to meet the first traceability analysis requirement which is to assure the design elements of concern are linked to at least one software element and the software elements are linked to at least one design element. Your solution will identify exactly HOW you are going to fulfill this requirement, which is dependent on the format of the developer's artifacts as well as the approach that you wish to take. If the developer's design is in a text document with diagrams and the source code is structured such that the function headers identify the design elements the particular function implements then you may choose to take a static analysis approach. The team would have to perform three V&V tasks to fulfill this requirement. First they would have to use a tool to extract the design element from the function headers. Secondly they would have to review the output from this extraction and determine if all of the design elements are linked to at least one software function. Thirdly they would have to identify if there are any software functions not related to at least one design element using the information provided by the extraction. This systems approach relies on defining the V&V requirements and then architecting a solution that meets the requirements. The Specifics for an actual solution are discussed in section 2.2.2 when we establish the V&V plan as well as in Chapter 3.

The last step of the planning process discussed in this book is that of scoping the system. You need to scope the system in order to identify the software components (e.g. subsystems, modules, functions) that will be assessed during the V&V effort. Basically you need to answer, what parts of the system need to be verified and validated in order to meet the objectives and goal for the project. You already know the requirements that you need to meet, but in order to meet the objectives what parts of the system have to be assessed. This is the scoping step.

You basically assess the software system against the objectives that you previously identified. For those software components that are related to the objectives, they become included in the scope of V&V. If the software component is not related to an objective then it is not part of the scope. We choose to use the project's system requirements to perform the scoping. One may be thinking ahead and wondering if you use the project's system requirements to identify the scope then how are you going to know what software requirements, software design elements, software code modules, and software test cases are within scope. I would reply with, you use a magic wand. No, just kidding, since you are performing full lifecycle V&V the traceability analysis requirements that the V&V team shall meet will establish the components that are related to the system functionality within scope. This cause-and-effect relationship will be used to guide

the V&V team to those components that require verification and validation. So let's use Project MUGSEY 0x01 again as an example along with
the second V&V objective:

*Provide assurance that the system software adequately identifies and
handles faults.*

We go through each system requirement and mark it as either being associated with the objective or not. So for MUGSEY's system requirements we determine that the following system requirements are associated
with the second V&V objective:

- Rquirement 3.4.3.1 Stored Commanding
- Requirement 6.3 Fault Handling
- Requirement 6.3.1 Science Faults
- Requirement 6.3.2 Abort Mission

These four items are the system functions that V&V must assess in order to meet one of their objectives. To do so, they will need to fulfill the
V&V system requirements stated in Table 2.2 and focus on the stored
commanding, fault handling, science faults, and abort mission system
functionality. Keep in mind this will only satisfy one of the objectives.
The scoping exercise needs to be performed for the other objectives as
well. As I stated before, traceability analysis will establish specifically
those software requirements, those design elements, those software elements, and those test elements associated with stored commanding, fault
handling, science faults, and abort mission functionality. The road map is
set for the V&V team and their requirements are established.

So let's take a moment and recap exactly what we have done for planning a V&V effort. The first thing to planning a V&V effort is to establish
the goal. The goal communicates the problem that is being solved by the
V&V team. It needs to be at an abstracted level in order to give some focus towards the development of objectives but it can't be too specific in
that it restricts the process and outcome. It is also a communications tool
for the V&V team and stakeholders to know what V&V is striving to accomplish.

Understanding the stakeholder's needs is the next essential step. These
will be used to help formulate the V&V objectives and possibly V&V requirements. The stakeholder's needs are used as input in generating V&V
objectives, V&V requirements, and the V&V concept.

The next crucial step is establishing the objectives for the V&V effort.
They are derived using the stakeholder requirements, the project's system
requirements, and the project's system needs. The objectives encapsulate

exactly what the V&V team is going to achieve. These objectives drive the scope of the V&V effort and possibly additional V&V requirements.

Next in the planning phase is the development of a V&V concept. This concept takes into account the possible organizational models the V&V team could assume, the interactions the V&V team will have with development, and potential artifacts the V&V team will be working with. Performing an assessment on the development artifacts that will be available to the V&V team is also essential during the planning phase. This will help the V&V team plan the concept as well as formulate solutions to the requirements. If they know the level of maturity the artifacts are going to be in or the type of format then different approaches can be used.

The last two steps can be performed in parallel. These steps are the development of the V&V requirements and the scope of the V&V effort. The V&V requirements are pre-defined and only require amending if the objectives call for it. The scope of the system that the V&V effort will focus on is a simple process of identifying what system functionality requires an assessment. This translates to identifying which system functions are associated with the established V&V objectives. The V&V team shall meet the V&V requirements by looking at the applicable system functionality, or the scope.

The results of these planning steps are depicted in Figure 2.4 and Figure 2.5. The goal, objectives, and the V&V scope is presented in Figure 2.4 and the V&V requirements are in Figure 2.5. These two figures represent the results of planning the V&V effort on Project MUGSEY 0x01. One note on the results is that one of the objectives, "Provide assurance that the system software is maintainable", is not represented in the scoping exercise but was added to the V&V requirements. Since maintenance aspects of the system are not related to just one system function it seems logical to add it as a requirement in order to fulfill the objective.

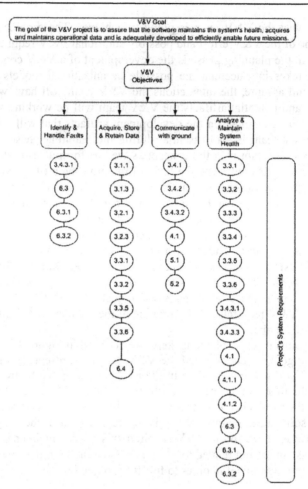

Fig. 2.4. Planning Results for the V&V Effort on Project MUGSEY 0x01.

Requirement No.	V&V Requirements
3.0	Functional Requirements
3.1	Traceability Analysis
3.1.1	V&V shall assure all the appropriate parent elements and child elements are in a relationship.
3.1.2	V&V shall assure that the parent elements are related to the right child elements.
3.1.3	V&V shall assure that relationships are consistent in their level of detail.
3.2	Interface Analysis
3.2.1	V&V shall assure that the right interface elements have been identified.
3.2.2	V&V shall assure all the interface elements are completely defined.
3.2.3	V&V shall assure that each interface element is used consistently.
3.2.4	V&V shall assure interface elements maintain the performance needs of the system.
3.2.5	V&V shall assure that interface elements are testable.
3.3	Technical Analysis
3.3.1	V&V shall assure the right child elements have been identified.
3.3.2	V&V shall assure the child element satisfies the parent element.
3.3.3	V&V shall assure the child elements are completely defined.
3.3.4	V&V shall assure that each child element is used consistently.
3.3.5	V&V shall assure the child element complies with appropriate standards and engineering practices.
3.3.6	V&V shall assure the logic and computational precision satisfy the needs of the system.
3.3.7	V&V shall assure all child elements are testable.
4.0	Nonfunctional Requirements
4.1	The V&V team shall minimize the amount of effort involved with the resolution of issues
4.2	The V&V team shall resolve issues with the development team
4.3	The V&V team shall develop and deliver a monthly status report to the Project Manager
4.4	The V&V team shall develop and deliver a technical report for each V&V task performed
4.5	The V&V team shall assure the software is maintainable.

Fig. 2.5. V&V Requirements for Project MUGSEY 0x01.

As you can see the systems approach to planning is very goal, objective, and requirements driven. It is easy to identify why V&V is assessing certain items as well as what they will achieve when they are complete. I truly advocate this approach but it is more time consuming as compared to the criticality approach defined in the next section. It is up to the V&V team to choose the approach they feel will provide them with the best plans to begin execution.

Section 2.2.1.2 Criticality Approach

To understand the approach outlined in the IEEE standard a concept needs to be introduced, which is the concept of a software integrity level (SIL)[2]. This concept is being reused from the IEEE standard. The premise is that different levels of integrity are used to describe the criticality of the software systems. Once that is accomplished, different sets of V&V tasks are performed for specific levels of integrity. This approach asserts that

---

[2] Software Integrity Level (SIL) is a concept that was first introduced in the IEEE Std 1012-1998. It is based on the fact that software components are either critical or not. The SIL established degrees of criticality and allows software components to be categorized based on their level of criticality.

higher levels of software integrity warrant more V&V tasks to be performed. In addition, integrity levels are assigned to specific software components, depending on which integrity level is assigned determines whether or not the software components fall within scope of V&V.

The approach is quite basic. The idea is to break the system down into software components. Components are user-defined and can be requirements, functions, groups of functions, components, or software subsystems. Since this planning is performed as early as possible, I have found that using the system requirements provides the best results.

After defining what a software component is for your project, you must define the approach for assigning a SIL to each software component. This simply means that the V&V team must identify the criterion that differentiates the levels of software integrity. The V&V team can reuse the definitions documented in the IEEE standard or create their own. Figure 2.6 presents the SIL definitions from IEEE.

IEEE Std. 1012-1998 Software Integrity Level Scheme		
Criticality	**Description**	**Level**
High	Selected function affects critical performance of the system	4
Major	Selected function affects important system performance	3
Moderate	Selected function affects system performance, but workaround strategies can be implemented to compensate for loss of performance	2
Low	Selected function has noticeable effect on system performance but only creates inconvenience to the user if the function does not perform in accordance with requirements.	1

Fig. 2.6. Software Integrity Level Definitions.

Once the V&V team agrees to the SIL definitions the team must identify the V&V tasks associated with each SIL. Again, the V&V team can use that already defined by IEEE or they can establish their own. Figure 2.7 presents an example of V&V tasking assigned to each SIL.

Phase	Tasks	Level 1	Level 2	Level 3	Level 4
	V&V Tasking	**Software Integrity Level (SIL)**			
Requirements V&V	Traceability Analysis		X	X	X
	Requirements Evaluation	X	X	X	X
	Interface Analysis		X	X	X
	System V&V Test Plan Generation & Verification			X	X
	System Test Plan Analysis	X	X		
	Acceptance V&V Test Plan Generation & Verification			X	X
	Acceptance Test Plan Analysis		X		
	Hazard Analysis			X	X
Design V&V	Traceability Analysis		X	X	X
	Design Evaluation	X	X	X	X
	Interface Analysis		X	X	X
	Componenet V&V Test Plan Generation & Verification			X	X
	Component Test Plan Analysis		X		
	Integration V&V Test Plan Generation & Verification			X	X
	Integration Test Plan Analysis	X	X		
	V&V Test Design Generation & Verification			X	X
	Test Design Analysis	X	X		
	Hazard Analysis			X	X
Implementation V&V	Traceability Analysis		X	X	X
	Source Code Evaluation	X	X	X	X
	Interface Analysis		X	X	X
	V&V Test Case Generation & Verification			X	X
	Test Case Analysis	X	X		
	V&V Test Procedure Generation & Verification			X	X
	Test Procedure Analysis	X	X		
	Component V&V Test Execution and Verification			X	X
	Component Test Results Analysis		X		
	Hazard Analysis			X	X
Test V&V	Traceability Analysis		X	X	X
	Acceptance V&V Test Procedure Generation & Verification			X	X
	Acceptance Test Procedure Analysis		X		
	Integration V&V Test Execution & Verification			X	X
	Integration Test Results Analysis	X	X		
	System V&V Test Execution & Verification			X	X
	System Test Results Analysis	X	X		
	Acceptance V&V Test Execution & Verification			X	X
	Acceptance Test Results Analysis		X		
	Hazard Analysis			X	X

Fig. 2.7. V&V Tasking per SIL level.

This simply means if a software component is considered to be a software integrity level of 1, then those tasks that have an X in the SIL column labeled "Level 1" are performed by the V&V Team. The function of planning is now an iterative loop that takes each software component and assesses it against the SIL definitions. This will result in a SIL assignment for each software component.

Consider the system requirements for project MUGSEY 0x01, depicted in Figure 2.8, as an example. The system requirements were assessed against the SIL definitions from Figure 2.6. The resulting SIL assignments per requirement are shown in the last column of Figure 2.8.

MUGSEY 0x01 System Requirements			SIL Assignment	
Number	Name	Description	Criticality	SIL
3.1.1	Imaging Frequency	Pictures during ascent and descent shall be obtained at a rate of at least one picture every minute.	High	4
3.1.2	Imaging Resolution	Pictures shall be of a resolution of 640 x 480.	Major	3
3.1.3	Imaging Stamp	Pictures shall be time-stamped with the local onboard time and position.	Moderate	2
3.2.1	Temperature Frequency	Temperature readings shall be taken at a frequency of at least once every 10 seconds.	High	4
3.2.2	Temperature Resolution	Temperature readings shall be in Fahrenheit with a precision of two decimal places.	Major	3
3.2.3	Temperature Stamp	Temperature readings shall be time-stamped with the local onboard time and position.	Moderate	2
3.3.1	Position Data	MUGSEY 0x01 shall obtain and store altitude, longitude, and latitude readings during ascent and descent.	High	4
3.3.2	Position Data Frequency	Position readings shall be taken at a frequency of at least once per 5 seconds.	High	4
3.3.3	Position Data Altitude Resolution	Altitude readings shall be taken in feet and with a precision of 2 decimal places.	Major	3
3.3.4	Position Data Position Resolution	Position readings shall be taken in degrees of longitude and latitude in this format (TBD) with a precision of 2 decimal places.	Major	3
3.3.5	Position Data Altitude Stamp	Altitude readings shall be time-stamped with the local onboard time and position.	Major	3
3.3.6	Position Data Position Stamp	Position readings shall be time-stamped with local onboard time and altitude.	Major	3
3.4.1	Telemetry	MUGSEY shall telemeter the position of the vehicle during ascent and descent to the ground segment.	High	4
3.4.3	Commanding	MUGSEY 0x01 shall be able to receive and process commands	Major	3
3.4.3.1	Stored Commanding	MUGSEY 0x01 shall process a command sequence upon entering a failure scenario.	Major	3
3.4.3.2	Real Time Commanding	MUGSEY 0x01 shall receive commands from the ground and process them within 10 seconds.	Moderate	2
3.4.3.3	Invalidate Commands	MUGSEY 0x01 shall invalidate a command if it is not recognized.	Low	1
4.1	Recovery Separation	MUGSEY 0x01 shall separate the observatory segment from the launch segment when commanded or when it reaches 50,000 feet in altitude.	Major	3
4.1.1	Recovery Separation Performance	Separation shall occur within 5 seconds of initiation	Low	1
4.1.2	Recovery Separation Parachute	Upon separation, MUGSEY 0x01 shall deploy a parachute	Major	3
4.1.3	Recovery Separation Strobe	Upon separation, MUGSEY 0x01 shall turn on the strobe light.	Moderate	2
5.0	Operations	MUGSEY 0x01 provides a ground segment for operations during ascent and descent.	Low	1
5.1	Receive Telemetry	MUGSEY 0x01 shall be able to receive all telemetry during ascent and descent.	Moderate	2
5.2	Commanding	MUGSEY 0x01 operations shall send commands during ascent and descent from the ground operations.	Moderate	2
6.3	Fault Handling	MUGSEY 0x01 shall recognize when its subsystems are not responding and recover them within 5 minutes.	Major	3
6.3.1	Science Faults	No failures in the system shall keep any of the science readings (images, temperature, altitude, and position) from being taken for no more than 5 minutes.	Major	3
6.3.2	Abort Missions	MUGSEY 0x01 shall recognize when it enters a hazardous zone and abort the mission.	Major	3
6.4	Data Loss	All data shall be retrieved from MUGSEY 0x01 with no data loss.	Major	3

Fig. 2.8. Example SIL Assignment for Project MUGSEY 0x01.

Now that each software component has been assigned an integrity level, it becomes an easy look up in the table to identify which V&V task should be performed on that component. Keep in mind, the resulting assignments of SILs were my own judgment and in practice would require a team of subject matter experts to assign the SIL level. The resulting Requirements

Phase V&V tasks that would be performed by the V&V team on Project MUGSEY 0x01 are depicted in Figure 2.9.

Reqt. No	System Requirement	SIL	Traceability Analysis	Requirements Analysis	Interface Analysis	Develop System V&V Test Plan and Analysis	System Test Plan Analysis	Develop Acceptance Test Plan and Analysis	Acceptance Test Plan Analysis	Hazard Analysis
3.1.1	Imaging Frequency	4	X	X	X	X		X		X
3.1.2	Imaging Resolution	3	X	X	X	X		X		X
3.1.3	Imaging Stamp	2	X	X	X		X		X	
3.2.1	Temperature Frequency	4	X	X	X	X		X		X
3.2.2	Temperature Resolution	3	X	X	X	X		X		X
3.2.3	Temperature Stamp	2	X	X	X		X		X	
3.3.1	Position Data	4	X	X	X	X		X		X
3.3.2	Position Data Frequency	4	X	X	X	X		X		X
3.3.3	Position Data Altitude Resolution	3	X	X	X	X		X		X
3.3.4	Position Data Position Resolution	3	X	X	X	X		X		X
3.3.5	Position Data Altitude Stamp	3	X	X	X	X		X		X
3.3.6	Position Data Position Stamp	3	X	X	X	X		X		X
3.4.1	Telemetry	4	X	X	X	X		X		X
3.4.3	Commanding	3	X	X	X	X		X		X
3.4.3.1	Stored Commanding	3	X	X	X	X		X		X
3.4.3.2	Real Time Commanding	2	X	X	X		X		X	
3.4.3.3	Invalidate Commands	1		X		X				
4.1	Recovery Separation	3	X	X	X	X		X		X
4.1.1	Recovery Separation Performance	1		X		X				
4.1.2	Recovery Separation Parachute	3	X	X	X	X		X		X
4.1.3	Recovery Separation Strobe	2	X	X	X		X		X	
5.0	Operations	1		X		X				
5.1	Receive Telemetry	2	X	X	X		X		X	
5.2	Commanding	2	X	X	X		X		X	
6.3	Fault Handling	3	X	X	X	X		X		X
6.3.1	Science Faults	3	X	X	X	X		X		X
6.3.2	Abort Missions	3	X	X	X	X		X		X
6.4	Data Loss	3	X	X	X	X		X		X

Column group header: Requirements V&V / V&V Tasks / MUGSEY 0x01 V&V Project

Fig. 2.9. Example V&V Tasking for Project MUGSEY 0x01.

As a result of this approach, the V&V team would perform Traceability Analysis for the majority of the system requirements, requirements analysis for all of the system requirements and interface analysis for the majority of the system requirements except for invalidating commands, recovery separation performance, and operations. The V&V team would assess the system test plans for a few of the requirements and they would develop system test plans for the remaining. The V&V team would assess the acceptance test plans for a few of the requirements and develop acceptance tests for the remaining. Lastly, the V&V team would perform hazard analysis on the majority of the system requirements. For the detailed descriptions of these tasks I refer you to Chapter 3.

IEEE also introduces another level to assess the software components against and that is the likelihood that an error would be inserted into the system. A combination between criticality and likelihood is then used to identify the tasks that shall be performed as well as the software components that fall within scope of the V&V tasks.

The most important thing to take away from this section is the fact that if you choose to use this planning approach then your documentation must be impeccable. Specifically state how your team is to define software components. These software components are the basis for your assessment. Next, be very clear on how the team is to assign software integrity levels. If using a combination of criticality and likelihood or just criticality, be sure that it is clearly documented what it means for a software component to be different levels of each. Next, identify the V&V tasks that are associated with the different software integrity levels. And lastly, when assigning software integrity levels, have your subject matter experts state their rationale for why they think that software component A is a high criticality or whatever the resultant criticality is. This rationale is essential for justifying why certain V&V tasks need to be performed as well as if the project reassesses the plan then they will need to understand why they are performing certain tasks.

As you can clearly see this approach is very basic and very straight forward. It incorporates a lot of engineering judgment that when repeated will most likely yield different results. This is why I can't stress enough that your project's documentation has to be flawless.

To conclude let's take a look at the differences between the systems engineering approach to planning and the criticality approach. There are three main differences that can be seen in the results. First, the systems engineering approach does not include the following system functions in their scope:

- Requirement 3.1.2 Imaging Resolution
- Requirement 3.4.3 Commanding
- Requirement 4.1.3 Recovery Separation Strobe
- Requirement 5.0 Operations

This simply means that the systems engineering approach has deemed that these system functions are not associated with any of the V&V objectives. As such, the V&V effort does not need to include them when performing their analysis.

The second difference is the systems approach has identified one system function that the criticality approach does not and that is requirement 3.4.2 "Data Dump". The systems approach has indicated that this functionality is important to the overall success of the mission and will include it in their scope when performing assessments.

The last difference is very significant. The systems approach focuses the V&V analysis according to the objectives they wish to achieve. For example, the systems approach will focus the V&V assessments on stored commanding, fault handling, science faults, and abort mission functionality with the objective of assuring that these functions can adequately identify when a fault is present and handle it appropriately. The resulting V&V effort from the systems approach is much focused and can be characterized as having more depth instead of breadth. As opposed to the criticality approach, this seems to provide more breadth than depth. This means that the criticality approach results in V&V efforts that take a broad brushed approach to finding issues. The V&V tasks are focused on finding issues, any issue anywhere. The systems approach; although may find issues, focuses on achieving an objective (e.g. assuring that fault handling is adequate for the system during operations).

Section 2.2.2 Establishing the V&V Plan

Attention needs to focus towards a solution now that the goal, objectives, requirements, and scope have been established. The solution shall reveal HOW the V&V team is going to meet the established requirements and objectives.

A network diagram is a very useful planning tool that will aid you in architecting a solution. The diagram is usually represented graphically and then displayed in its normal form of a Gantt chart. For example, we have used Project MUGSEY 0x01 numerous times and I will refer back to it now.

I will use the V&V requirements for Interface Analysis as an example for laying out a solution. Let's refresh, the V&V requirements for Interface Analysis are depicted in Table 2.3.

Table 2.3. V&V Requirements for Interface Analysis.

V&V Requirement No.	Title	V&V Requirement
3.2	Interface Analysis	
3.2.1		V&V shall assure that the right interface elements have been identified.
3.2.2		V&V shall assure all the interface elements are completely defined.
3.2.3		V&V shall assure that each interface element is used consistently.
3.2.4		V&V shall assure interface elements maintain the performance needs of the system.
3.2.5		V&V shall assure that interface elements are testable.

During the requirements phase, the V&V team shall provide assurance that the software interfaces adequately support the identification and handling of faults (the second V&V objective). The project's system requirements that V&V needs to assess are stored commanding, fault handling, science faults, and abort mission requirements. A network diagram needs to be developed that meets those 5 interface analysis requirements. Table 2.4 identifies the V&V tasks that need to be performed to meet the Interface Analysis requirements. These tasks will then be used to develop the network diagram and project schedule. As a side note, it may not be clear as to how I came up with the V&V tasks. For the purposes of discussing planning let's just assume that the tasking is adequate and concentrate on the planning steps. We will readdress the specific V&V tasking and possible approaches in Chapter 3.

Table 2.4. Set of V&V Tasks to fulfill Interface Analysis requirements.

V&V Task	V&V Requirement Fulfilled	V&V Approach	Duration Days (Min, Avg., Max)
Identify a set of potential faults	None	Static Analysis {Use Cases and Scenarios}	(1,2,3)
Identify the interfaces required to identify and handle these faults	None	Static Analysis {Use Cases and Scenarios}	(2,4,6)
Identify the data items that	None	Static Analysis	(3,7,10)

		{Use Cases and	
should be passed between interfaces		Scenarios}	
Compare and contrast the results with the system and software interface requirements	3.2.1	Manual Analysis	(5,7,12)
Determine if each data item is completely defined	3.2.2	Manual Analysis	(1,3,5)
Graph the locations of each data item and determine if they are used consistently	3.2.3	Static Analysis	(2,7,12)
Add temporal properties to the data items and simulate transactions	3.2.4	Dynamic Analysis	(7,14,24)
Develop test cases data items and fault scenarios and determine if any of them can not be tested.	3.2.5	Static Analysis	(2,3,4)

The first column in Table 2.4 depicts the V&V task. The second column identifies which Interface Analysis requirement is being met by the V&V task. The third column represents the approach that is to be taken when implementing the V&V task. The four possible approaches are manual analysis, static analysis, dynamic analysis, and formal analysis. These are discussed more in Chapter 3 when we discuss the V&V life cycle. The last column represents the amount of time needed to perform the V&V task. The values represent the minimum amount of time, the average amount of time, and the maximum amount of time. This is when the experience and knowledge of the SMEs is crucial. Management and SMEs have to work together in order to come up with an adequate approach to performing V&V. The reason for the 3 different values for duration is that most management groups use simulation as a management technique. They will perform Monte Carlo simulations on the tasking to determine which tasks affect the overall project the most and which ones you could possibly change that would have the greatest impact. It also leads to some very interesting "What If" strategies that management can use to control the project. These values are also used to generate cost estimates. Again, these are pretty standard techniques and I leave you to your favorite management 101 book for more discussions.

This data is used to develop the network diagram. This is where the logical relationships are established between tasks as well as duration and resources. Figure 2.10 depicts a portion of the network diagram that represents the tasks in Table 2.4. A network diagram is essential for planning a

V&V project. If you have never used a network diagram or cannot build a network diagram then stop all of you management activities and take a lesson in project management 101. It will surely cover the development of network diagrams. They are so simple to build and are often overlooked by management. Figure 2.10 shows an example network diagram and Figure 2.11 shows the project schedule for the V&V effort on MUGSEY 0x01.

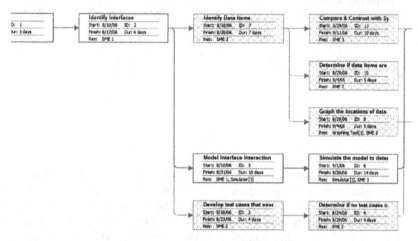

Fig. 2.10. Example Network Diagram for MUGSEY V&V Project.

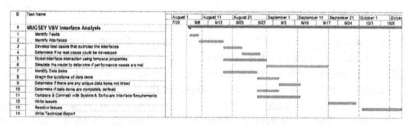

Fig. 2.11. Example Schedule for MUGSEY V&V Project.

The network diagram in Figure 2.10 is used to generate the schedule that you see in Figure 2.11. These tasks are those that are needed to be performed by the V&V team in order to fulfill the interface analysis requirements. As I stated before, from here on out the planning steps are standard management practices that appear in your favorite management books. If they are new to you and you have management responsibilities for the V&V project then maybe you should book mark this section and come back to it when you get up to speed on these approaches. The last step in the planning process is to develop the project plan. This is simply compiling all of the data, discussed thus far, into one document.

Table 2.5 presents the topics that need to be addressed in the V&V Project Plan. The paragraphs that follow Table 2.5 provide more detail. How the V&V Project Plan is organized is not of concern to me. What I am concerned about is the content of the plan. At a minimum the plan needs to cover the topics outlined in Table 2.5.

Table 2.5. Topics to be addressed in the V&V Project Plan.

Project Plan Topic	Description
Overview	Describe the system that V&V is to work on. In addition, identify the V&V goal, V&V stakeholders and their requirements, and V&V objectives.
References	Identify any artifacts used to generate the plan as well as define any acronyms or terms that make the plan understandable.
V&V Concept	Identify the organizational approach the V&V team is employing as well as how the team is going to interact with the development project. Roles and responsibilities need to be identified.
Schedule	Either present the master schedule in the plan or reference the external file.
Resources	Discuss the resources required to execute the V&V plan.
Technical Scope of Work	Discuss the scope of work to be performed by the V&V team as well as the approach taken to derive the technical approach. If you use the systems engineering approach then this is where you discuss the V&V requirements and V&V scope.
Tools and Methods	Identify any tools that are needed to execute the V&V plan or special methods that will be used.
V&V Management Approach	Discuss the management of V&V including control measures, risk management approach, issue management approach, and the reporting requirements that V&V shall follow.
V&V Life Cycle	Discuss the life cycle for the V&V effort detailing the V&V tasks that need to be performed and how they are going to fulfill the V&V requirements.

An overview of the V&V project consists of identifying the goal of the V&V effort and its objectives. This section shall identify the system to which the plan applies as well as the specific parts of the software system that falls within scope and those that fall out of scope. So for example, Project MUGSEY 0x01, it may be that the ground system is not within scope of the V&V effort to which this plan would not be applicable. The overview section needs to make it very clear as to what V&V shall achieve and what it takes to be considered successful. The technical scope of work is also addressed later on in the plan. In the overview it just needs to be stated as to what parts of the system this plan is applicable.

Other items of information that may be included in the overview or be separate include referenced documents, definitions and acronyms. This information is used to identify the documents used or referenced in the plan as well as used during the implementation of the project. The acronyms and definitions serve to assure a proper interpretation of the plan, which includes identifying and spelling out all acronyms and notations that are used.

The V&V concept needs to clearly show the V&V organization, roles and responsibilities and how the V&V project interacts with the development project. Specific items that shall be addressed include:

- Define the organization of the V&V effort, relationship to other efforts and entities, as well as lines of communication.
- Identify the authority for resolving issues.
- Identify the authority for approving V&V products.
- Identify the authority for making any changes to the plan.
- Identify the responsibilities for each element in the organization.

The master schedule can be an external reference or embedded in the plan. The schedule is a living document and will change as the V&V project is implemented. The master schedule shall address the following topics:

- Summarize the various V&V tasks and their relationships within the overall project environment.
- The objective is to spell out the orderly flow of artifacts between V&V activities and project tasks. This helps ensure that V&V tasks are appropriately placed and their deliverables are identified within the larger project environment.
- Focus on the V&V tasks and their placement within the project schedule and highlight the V&V tasks, deliverables, and completion dates.

The resources needed to implement the V&V tasks shall be identified in their own section. More than likely it will be a bottoms-up estimate developed from the work packages and the identified risks. This section shall summarize the resources needed to perform the V&V tasks, including staffing, facilities, tools, finances, and special requirements (e.g. security access, documentation control).

The next section shall identify the approach taken to establish the V&V requirements. It describes the scheme for identifying V&V tasks and their scope. This can reference external technical reports that provide the details of the process; however, a summary needs to be included in the plan.

The tools and methods section shall identify the required resources needed to implement the V&V tasks. Identify the tools, techniques, and methods employed by the V&V effort. The purpose and use of each shall be described. Include the following information when discussing tools and methods:

- A description of, or reference to, the methodology.
- Risks associated with a tool or technique.
- Alternate approaches.

The V&V management section of the plan needs to address actions to be taken by management during the implementation of the V&V effort. For the management of V&V actions that need to be considered and addressed include how the V&V project is going to respond to a change in the technical scope of the project they are V&V'ing. The control measures that are to be used by management to assure that the V&V objectives are being met as well as the schedule and budget are on track. Tools that management can use include control gates (e.g. management reviews), earned-value, or effectiveness measures. All of these topics are discussed in greater detail later in this chapter.

The risk management approach shall also be addressed in the management section. The topics that shall be addressed in the project plan include:

- Define the risk management approach.
- Identify the method of reporting and resolving risks as well as the distribution list.
- Define the criticality levels used to categorize risks.
- Define the tracking process and any tools that will be used.

Issue management, just like risk management, needs to be clearly articulated in the plan. The details for how issues are communicated, resolved, as well as who has the authority to close issues is essential to the successful management of any V&V effort. This leads into the last topic of the management section and that is the reporting requirements. The purpose of the reporting requirements information is to communicate what is produced by the V&V project and its format. The other critical piece of information regarding V&V reporting is the contents of the report. Clearly identify what the contents of each of the reports are to contain and when they will be produced.

The last topic of the project plan needs to address the specific V&V tasks that are to be performed on the project. You also need to assure that they do not contradict any of the information already presented in the plan (e.g. master schedule). For each of the V&V tasks, the information in Table 2.6 needs to be addressed.

Table 2.6. Topics to Be Addressed for Each V&V Task

Topic	Description
Associated Requirement	Identify the V&V requirement(s) that the task fulfills.
Objectives or Rationale	Identify the expected outcomes or explain how the task fulfills the associated V&V requirement(s).
Tools and Methods	Describe the tools and/or methods that will be used to perform the task.
Input	Identify the required inputs for the task along with whom or what will provide it and the required format of each input.
Scope	Identify the software components that will be assessed by this task.
Output	Identify the required outputs from each task, their purpose, format, and recipients.
Schedule	Identify the schedule for each task, establishing specific milestones for initiating and completing each task.
Resources	Identify the resources needed to perform the task.
Risks and Assumptions	Identify any risks or assumptions and provide recommendations to eliminate or mitigate.
Effectiveness Profile	Identify the defect profile to which this task will be assessed against.

Section 2.3 Managing the Plan

During implementation the management team has several tools at their disposal to assure they meet their plans within the +10% and -5% margins established at the onset of the project. The actual management of the project takes on tasks such as planning, input analysis, risk management, issue management, reporting, controlling the project, and change assessments.

As I have stated before, this book is not entirely focused on management techniques. I simply discuss those techniques that I feel must be performed if you want to be successful.

For example, planning has been discussed in the previous sections. The one important point that I wish to make is that planning is not a one time event and plans must be continuously assessed throughout the life of the project.

Input analysis is also discussed in the previous sections and is important when laying out plans. In order to plan effectively you must be aware of the environment that you have to operate in. V&V must also understand the type of artifacts as well as there maturity when deciding on their approaches.

Issue and risk management is discussed in subsequent sections. An additional point that I would like to make in this section regarding issue management is that issue resolution is extremely difficult to plan for. The resolution of issues is difficult to plan as well as control. As such, I have found it advantageous to build reserve into the schedule to cover an extensive use of resources to resolve issues.

Reporting is discussed in various sections in the book, from the possible organizational structures the V&V team may employ to the contents of the V&V plan.

Control techniques are introduced in the following sections. The new concepts that are discussed are effectiveness measures and control gates. I have some concern if I don't discuss earned value management. Since it is not a new technique I lessen the concern but not completely. Earned value management has proven to be a very successful management tool in the development community and has been successful in the V&V community although in limited instances. Even though it is not a new concept I briefly mention it in the trailing paragraphs.

Change assessment is a management task that has to be performed every time the development project makes a change to any of their artifacts. Either a change to an artifact that has already been analyzed by V&V or a change to future artifacts, management has to understand what the change impacts with respect to the V&V results and the V&V plans. It is possible for the development project to change a requirement. Imagine a world where requirements are not changed once they are baselined, pretty good imagination if you were able to see it. As such, if a requirement changes and the V&V team has already assessed the requirements and the requirement is in scope then management needs to understand whether or not their previous results have been affected. You need to plan for these changes. Just like issue management, changes to the development artifacts

can wreak havoc on your V&V plans. These are those uncontrollable variables that everyone writes about and discusses.

I leave you now with a few thoughts on earned value. Consider a project in which you are building brake pads for an automobile manufacturer.
Can you somehow put in place a measurement system that gives you the
insight that not only enables you to determine the current state of production but will enable you to make predictions about the future production of
your brake pads? Does this sound to good to be true? Well it is and that is
all I want to say about earned value. I guess I'll retract that last statement
so that you'll read on.

Earned value is a tool, just a tool, and it is one that you must fully understand if you are going to use it. If you don't understand what it is and
how the numbers are generated then you can make some very serious mistakes, ill-informed decisions would soon follow. But when it is understood
it can be effectively applied to the V&V project which will allow management the insight into the current state of the analysis as well as predict
whether or not it is going to meet its plans. With enough granularity it will
even allow you to determine what the root causes of the problems are so
that effective remedies can be put in place.

I can not do earned value management enough justification with just a
few paragraphs nor could I if I devoted a section or even a chapter to it.
Entire books have been written on this management technique and I am
not about to recite everything they do. I refer you to the latest management books that exist to teach the basics of earned value. What I will say
about earned-value management is that it can be used effectively on a
V&V project. Once the mentality of V&V becomes requirements driven
then earned-value can be used effective. Two things need to be taken into
consideration when applying earned-value to your project. First, you have
to be requirements driven. Your mentality has to become centered on the
fact that V&V produces something. And they do, just because they perform assessments does not indicate a level of effort. Performing an assessment still results in a tangible product that can be measured and moni-
tored. The other thing to consider is the fact that V&V is totally dependent
on the developer's schedule. For example, V&V can establish a Budgeted
Cost of Work Scheduled (BCWS) for performing their interface analysis
tasks but if the developer is late in providing the interface requirements
then V&V is going to show a negative schedule variance. The insight into
these scenarios, which is common, would be meaningless. You know that
you are slipping your schedule if you haven't been given the required input. This makes earned-value a re-planning exercise every time the developer's are late. I can't argue with these scenarios because I have seen
them happen to often. Although I will say that you do need to address

your plans if you can not meet your schedule. If earned-value is deemed nothing more than a re-planning exercise then you should take a hard look at your management system. This would tell me that your management system is not robust enough to incorporate changes and we all know that projects will experience changes. A management approach as well as a management system that can handle change will be successful. Ones that are not, well then I understand the attitude they have towards earned-value.

Section 2.3.2 Effectiveness Measures

Another new concept introduced in this book has to deal with using effectiveness measures to manage the V&V tasks. The concept is not new to the software engineering community; it is new to the V&V community. One of the problems that haunt a V&V team is knowing when they are done verifying and validating a system component. This is very similar to the question "How do you know when you are done inspecting source code?" There seems to be an effective approach to answering this question. I say that it seems to be effective for two reasons; first I have tried the approach a few times and it provided valuable insight and second, industry has tried the approach within the development organization and published papers find it favorable.

The concept is based on Orthogonal Defect Classification (ODC) and was introduced by IBM in the early 1970s (Fagan 1976). First we need to discuss the act of modeling a process (a V&V task). No process can be modeled as an observable and controllable system unless explicit input/output or cause-and-effect relationships are established. When cause-and-effect is recognized, though qualitatively, it is not abstracted to a level from which it could graduate to engineering models. ODC bridges the gaps between quantitative methods and qualitative analysis by bringing in scientific methods that define a measurement system in an area that has been historically ad hoc. It does better than raw counts of defects by using the semantic information contained within.

Let's step back and make sure we understand the problem we are trying to solve. As an example, consider a V&V team performing test analysis on the project's test cases. The V&V team assesses the test cases to assure that they are adequately covering the software requirements. When the V&V team is finished there are several entities of knowledge that have been generated. First, the V&V team has possibly identified issues with the test cases. Second, the V&V team has possibly achieved their objectives and third, the V&V team has gained valuable knowledge about the system by itself. The challenge that management has is deciding whether or not the V&V team is done and their results complete. Can management conclude that if the V&V team has met their objectives then they are done with test analysis? If the V&V team have generated 50 issues is that enough? To answer this, management needs a combination of techniques that enables them to assess their own processes and determine the level of quality that has been achieved when performing them.

Now let's get back to ODC and how it can be used as a management tool. This may seem like a Quentin Tarantino movie, jumping back and forth between scenarios but I find it important to make sure we were clear with the problem that we are trying to solve. ODC exploits defects that occur all the way through development cycle. It converts semantically rich defect data into a few vital measurements on the product and process. These measurements provide a firm footing upon which sophisticated analysis and methodologies are developed. ODC's success illustrated that a new class of methods can be developed that rely on semantic extraction of information linking the qualitative aspects from root-cause analysis to measurable computable aspects from statistical defect models (Chillarege 1996). The semantic extraction is done via classification. The objectives are to contrast the classical methods of growth modeling with what can be achieved via semantic extraction from defects.

One approach that V&V could take is a reliability approach and model the growth rate of defects they uncover. Once the growth curve has seemed to stabilize, or reach a plateau, then in combination with the assessment on the quality of the test cases one can determine whether or not the system is going to experience any more defects. Meaning, the V&V team could look for more defects but the growth model indicates that no more would be found that would be beneficial for the resources expended. Consider the example growth model depicted in Figure 2.12. Ideally the graph should plateau, signifying a decreasing number of defects being detected and promising fewer defects in the field. The sudden increase in the defect rate, during the time period of 900 days, identifies the criticality of the situation. Classical growth curve modeling techniques would recognize this trend and identify it as a problem. However, the problem with this is that it would be recognized too late to take all but some desperate reactive measures, unless the modeling technique used some comparison function that determined when the slope of the line deviates from some predetermined stability value. However, employing a technique such as that would only raise a flag, it would not identify the potential cause of the problem nor would it motivate corrective measures.

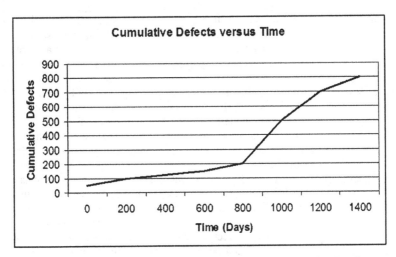

Fig. 2.12. Example growth model for defects experienced during the development life cycle

ODC's classification system relies on several attributes but the two used by the V&V team could be defect type and defect trigger. The V&V team would need to categorize the defects they find using the class types defined in Table 2.7.

Table 2.7. Defect Types for a V&V project.

Defect Type	Description	Example
Function	The error requires a formal change to the software artifact, as it affects significant capability.	Requirements for a significant subsystem are missing
Assignment	Value(s) assigned incorrectly or not assigned at all.	Internal variable or variable within a control block did not have correct value, or did not have any value at all
Interface	Communication problems between modules, components, device drivers, objects, functions vi macros, call statements, control blocks, or parameter lists.	The interface specifies a pointer to a number, but the implementation is expecting a pointer to a character
Checking	Errors caused by missing or incorrect validation of parameters or data in conditional statements. Also refers to test cases that do not validate certain measures.	Test case doesn't check the frequency rate only the message content

Timing	Necessary serialization of shared resource was missing, the wrong resource was serialized, or the wrong serialization technique was employed.	A hierarchical locking scheme is in use, but the code failed to acquire the locks in the prescribed sequence.
Relationship	Problems related to associations among procedures, data structures, objects, requirements, and tests.	Traceability from requirements to test is in error or missing.
Build	Errors that occur due to mistakes in library systems, management of changes, or version control.	The test environment is using the wrong tables during flight testing
Documentation	Information within documentation is inaccurate or missing and requires information to be added or changed.	Function does not have sufficient commenting or it does not describe the code accurately.
Algorithm	Efficiency or correctness problems that affect the task and can be fixed by (re)implementing an algorithm or local data structure without the need for requesting a design change. Problem in the test procedure where it doesn't fully verify the requirement	The algorithm for searching a chain of control blocks was corrected to use a linear-linked list instead of a circular-linked list.
Project	Requires revisiting the schedule, resources, and/or number of reviews.	Development teams are being tasked beyond their capability
Verification Method	The identified methods of verification are not explained or are not appropriate for the situation.	The Test Plan states that testing and demonstration are used to verify a certain requirement and analysis shows that both methods are not required.

The classes in Table 2.7 capture the essence of what was fixed. Semantically it represents the nature of the work necessary to fix the defect. As such, a V&V analyst when she finds an issue would then need to wait and see how the developer's fixed the issue. Or she could go ahead and make the classification based on what she thinks it would take to fix the issue. A note to the reader is that these defect types were synthesized from published papers and two projects that I used the technique on. These types may need to be modified for your project.

In addition to assigning a defect to a defect type class, V&V will also need to assign the same defect to a defect trigger class. The trigger is what facilitated the defect to surface. Ideally the trigger represents the V&V task being performed when the defect was found. The three classes of triggers defined by ODC are inspection, unit/function test, and system test. There are sub-classes within each of these that helps associate the activity the individual was doing to surface the defect. What is important at this point in time is to clearly define the V&V tasks for your organization. I am not going to regurgitate the triggers that ODC defines simply because they will more than likely not have any meaning to your organization. The defect trigger classes that your V&V organization will come up with will follow from the V&V requirements defined in this book.

Having these two separate classification schemes are used collectively to point to the part of the process that needs attention, much like characterizing a point in a Cartesian system of orthogonal axes by its x, y, and z coordinates (Chillarege 1996). This knowledge is also used to infer whether or not the V&V team has found what they thought they should have found. It is by no means binary and performed in vacuum. So let me reiterate that last line for management folks reading this book. These are simply indicators and it will require further exploration to reveal the root cause.

Once the defects are placed in their appropriate classes, we examine how the distribution contributed by defects changes as a function of time. Consider the example in Figure 2.13, which shows the proportion of defects that have the defect type "Function" during each development period. This example was taken from (Chillarege 1996). It simply shows when the development project identified defects of the type function. The early periods of development, periods 0-2 in this example, are characterized by larger amounts of design, whereas the latter parts, periods 2-3.5, are characterized by greater amounts of implementation and system test. Thus, the expectation would be that the proportion of defects of type function would be initially larger and smaller later. However, in this example we are not experiencing this. It is showing that we are revealing more function defects as we age in the development life cycle, hence the crisis. Instead of relying on raw defect counts, we could identify possible reasons for this phenomenon and apply corrective measures now, not later.

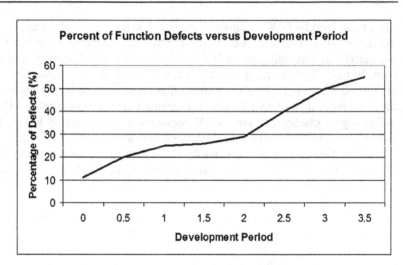

Fig. 2.13. Proportion of Function defect types during development.

The V&V team can use the same philosophy as development. If the V&V team experienced a similar defect distribution as in Figure 2.13, then management should assess why the V&V team did not find those design-like issues earlier on. Management could also make a decision to not continue on and reassess whether or not their objectives were met when assessing the design artifacts. This example showed an "after-the-fact" type of assessment and that is not what I am advocating here. I simply used the example to try to convey the concept of using defect type distributions to gauge whether or not the V&V team found what they thought they should find. The actual implementation of this technique is performed in step with the V&V task so that remedies can be deployed as potential problems arise.

The defect type's granularity is such that the classifications apply to a defect found in any phase of the development process, yet can be associated with a few specific activities in a particular process. For example, a typical association that occurs is to tie the functional defect type to the design process, thus no matter where the defect is found, if the distribution peaks, it is indicative of an activity that escaped the design phase. Similarly, an assignment or checking defect may be associated with the coding phase and is expected to be weeded out with code inspections and unit-test type activities. The previous example illustrated the use of qualitative information in defects converted to a quantitative measure to make earlier predictions than more traditional quantitative methods. In addition, it provides clues to the reasons, which are translatable to recommendations for action.

The elements belonging to the set of defect types are different enough that they span the development process. Given this set of defect types, there are several opportunities for determining effectiveness based on the profiles of the defect type distribution. V&V teams can exploit the defect type by generating the distribution of the defect types in each phase of V&V. Given a V&V phase one can describe the expected behavior. For instance, as I have stated previously the function defects should be found early in the process and ideally very few at system test. On the other hand, timing/serialization defects are found during system test. Assignment and interface defects can have profiles that peak at unit-test and integration test, respectively. Figure 2.14 is an example of an expected defect type distribution that could be used to gauge the results of a V&V task.

Issue Type	Requirements	HLD	LLD	Code	Unit Test	Function Test	System Test
Function	X	X				X	
Interface	X		X		X		X
Checking				X	X		X
Assignment	X			X			
Relationship	X			X			
Timing			X				X
Algorithm				X	X	X	X
Build							
Documentation	X						
Project		X					
Verification Method	X	X					

Fig. 2.14. Example Defect Type Distribution

The concept is to examine the normalized distribution of all defects found while performing a V&V task against what the process should achieve. This instrument will allow us to measure the progress of a product as well as the effectiveness of the analysis through the process. A departure from the expected distribution or a change from the expected trend identifies potential problems and recommends possible corrective action.

I have applied this technique during one of my V&V projects that I was managing in the past. The measurements were taken while we were performing test analysis in which test artifacts were being inspected for defects. Development was in the system-testing phase when we came on board, so no prior V&V tasks had been performed. We inspected software test plans, test procedures, test cases, test scripts, and requirement specifications and our defect type classes were used to characterize the defects that surfaced. We used the defect type distribution profile as depicted in Figure 2.14 and prior to performing our V&V task the team had concurred that the majority of the defects that we should find should be of type Interface. The second type should be checking, and the third type should be timing. We also felt that we may find some algorithm type defects simply because the actual test cases were being revealed for the first time and had not gone through any type of inspection. Since they were just being developed we felt we should uncover some problems on how well the requirements were being logically tested.

As we performed our analysis we began categorizing the defects that we found. Prior to completing the analysis our defect distribution was that depicted in Figure 2.15.

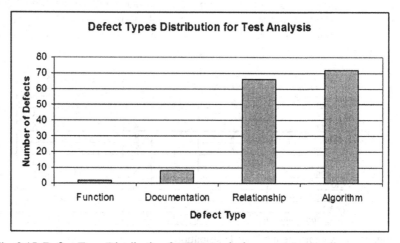

Fig. 2.15. Defect Type Distribution for Test Analysis

1.35% of the defects were of type function. Although it is a relatively small amount, it shows that these defects escaped the requirements and design phases and laid dormant until System Testing. 5.41% of the defects were of type documentation. This came as no surprise since we were inspecting documents for clarity and consistency. However, they should not have escaped the requirements and design phases since they were test plans and should have already been inspected. 44.59% of the defects were of type relationship, which are associated with the traceability of requirements to test procedures/cases and relationship characteristics between test plans and test procedures. Full coverage, as well as consistent flow between test documentation should have been well established before System Testing. 48.65% of the defects were of type algorithm, which is associated with the logic contained within the test cases that determines whether the requirements are fully, partially, or not at all verified by the test case.

These types of defects do not normally surface, if one is inspecting test artifacts, until unit test, function test, or System Test. Hence, the amount of defects that surfaced is indicative of the expected defect profile.

The concern was that we had deviated drastically from our expected defect profile. We met our schedule, came in on cost, and we had assessed all of the test cases, plans, etcetera. Now we were concerned that our analysis may not have been as best as we had intentionally hoped for. The lack of interface type defects, checking type defects, and timing type defects is what we were questioning.

First, we held a team meeting and discussed the possibilities. This being one of my first projects I found it extremely beneficial to hear the other seasoned analysts discuss how they assessed test cases for interface type defects. It quickly occurred to me that I did not take into consideration anything that they had mentioned. As we discussed this as a team, we found that the lack of direction on "How To" assess test cases that verify interfaces was lacking. That systems perspective was what I was lacking, as well as a couple others on the team. Our approaches varied and we were able to regroup and look at the test cases that I was responsible for looking at in the first place. This may come as a surprise to some that I am writing about my own failures but I am a firm believer that we learn as much from our mistakes as we do our failures. As such, it is okay to admit when you think or you know that you have made a mistake. It is not okay to cover it up. Since we had assessed our performance early on, we were able to readdress the test cases and still meet our schedule.

Checking type defects are associated with test cases verifying absolute measures defined in the requirements. There are a few possible reasons we did not find any defects of this type: If the requirements never stated any absolute measures in the specification then there would be no need to test them. Maybe our team didn't have the right skill mix, like I discussed in the previous paragraph, or maybe the right skill mix was there but the team deviated from their original focus. Lastly, maybe the tests covered everything they needed to and there weren't any defects to find.

We went back to the requirement specification and verified that the requirements do contain some absolute measures. So the first reason could be thrown out, as a result of the team meeting I discussed earlier we also concurred that we all took a very similar approach to assessing the test cases. That was when it became evident want went wrong, we all took a similar approach but the approach had deviated from our original intent.

What had occurred was that our V&V plans did not specifically detail the objectives for our test analysis activities. As such, our assessment of the test cases was ad hoc. It was successful in our eyes simply because the objectives were not very clear, it's hard to fail when the objectives are not clear. The testing of exact measures had simply slipped through our analysis "checklist", I quoted the word checklist because we didn't actually use a checklist. Even though there were a few requirements that stated absolute measures, our team had simply over looked them.

The last concern was that we had not found any timing type defects. After our team meeting we were confident that we had covered the timing properties stated in the requirements. It just so happened that the test cases also covered the timing properties and there were no defects to be found.

This was a perfect example of the success for in-process measurement. Before we closed out this task we refocused our analysis and made sure the test cases verified the interfaces as well as absolute measures defined in the requirements. The biggest lesson learned was that which spawned the writing of this book. As you read the previous paragraphs you may have been distraught with the facts that our V&V approaches were very ad hoc and totally dependent on the people performing the analysis. It was quickly realized that more formal definitions for performing V&V were needed. That is why I advocate defining, very clearly, what the objectives are BEFORE performing the task as well as laying out the approach so that all team members are very clear in knowing what it is they are expected to achieve as well as how they are to go about it.

This technique was beneficial in the two cases that I applied it. Even though I lack an exhaustive set of test data for it, I believe that coupled with standard management techniques it will provide additional insight into the quality of the V&V analysis that is being performed.

Section 2.3.3 Control Gates

It is absurd to think that only the development projects should have control gates. As a project manager, we must be just as rigorous when managing a V&V project as we are when managing a development project. Control gates are usually established at logical places in the life-cycle in order to assure the engineering aspects of the system being developed are maturing as expected. For example, the development team must go through a design review in order to show that they have a stable design that meets the requirements. It is the intent of the design review to enable the development team to begin implementing the design. Why is it so ludicrous to have the V&V team go through similar gates? For example, when the V&V team indicates they have completed design analysis, I feel they should show that they have completed all of their requirements for design analysis, that they have all tools in place to begin code analysis, all personnel are adequately trained, all risks have been managed adequately and the necessary issues have been resolved.

This is a completely new idea for V&V projects and I expect it to be a difficult one to start. I do not understand why it would be difficult to accept but I do understand that implementing this new concept would probably receive some push back, simply because it is a change in the way things are normally conducted.

The life cycle for a V&V project is modeled after the one chosen for the development project to assure timely feed back of the V&V results. No matter the life cycle chosen and disregarding the temporal aspects of the V&V phases (e.g. ignoring the start and end times for the tasks) control gates are established prior to the completion of these major V&V phases:

- Requirements Analysis
- Design Analysis
- Implementation Analysis
- Test Analysis

Prior to the completion of each of these phases, the control gates are used as critical decision points in the life of the V&V project. The control gates are a management function and serve as an excellent tool to make intelligent decisions. They are represented by formal reviews that are held by a review panel comprised of either management personnel separate from the V&V team, management from the V&V team, or both. For the current phase of the life-cycle, the review shall address the topics depicted in Figure 2.16.

Current V&V Task	
Review Topic	Description
Objectives	Have the objectives been met?
Issues	Have the necessary issues been communicated to the project?
	Have the necessary issues been resolved?
	Are there plans in place to resolve the issues in an adequate time-frame?
Risks	Have the necessary risks been managed adequately?
Effectiveness Models	What were the results of the effectiveness models?
	Are the results acceptable?
	If the results are not acceptable, what are the actions planned to be taken?
Results	Have the results of the V&V task been communicated to the project?
	How did the project respond or use the V&V results?
Lessons Learned	Have there been any lessons learned documented?
Schedule	Have you met your planned schedule?
Cost	Have you met your planned budget?

Fig. 2.16. Review Topics for Current V&V phase.

The topics depicted in Figure 2.16 can be used as a checklist by the V&V project as well as the review panel. For example, for the current

V&V phase the V&V project shall address the objectives and requirements that were to be met at completion of the phase and whether or not they were.

For the upcoming phase that the V&V team will perform, the review shall address the topics the depicted in Figure 2.17.

Review Topic	Upcoming V&V Task
	Description
Objecitves	Have the objectives been clearly defined?
Methods	Have the methods been clearly defined?
	Are the methods acceptable to meet the objectives?
Training	Are the appropriate V&V team members adequately trained in the methods?
Tools	Are the necessary tools installed, configured, and ready for operation?
Artifacts	Have the necessary development artifacts been made available to the V&V team?
	Are the artifacts in the proper format and mature enough to accomplish the objectives?
Issues	What issues are being carried forward?
	Have you planned to resolve any issues during the upcoming task?
Risks	What risks are being managed for the upcoming task?
Effectiveness Models	What are the effecitveness models planned to be used for the upcoming task?
Lessons Learned	What lessons learned have you used in planning for the upcoming task?
Schedule	Is the planned schedule adequate to meet the objectives?
Cost	Is the planned budget adequate to meet the objectives?

Fig. 2.17. Review Topics for Upcoming V&V phase.

Just like in Figure 2.16, the topics depicted in Figure 2.17 can be used as a checklist by the V&V project as well as the review panel. It is essential that these topics are addressed prior to the start of the V&V phase, it is management's responsibility to assure the success of the V&V phase and these topics serve as a guide to enable that success.

These reviews shall be planned for and integrated into the overall estimate for the V&V project. As I suggested in the preliminary paragraphs, the concept for V&V projects to go through reviews will not be accepted with open arms. As such, V&V management should at least informally address these topics within their team to assure they are staying on track and meeting the needs of the overall V&V project.

Section 2.4 Risk Management

The future is our concern and management can not plan a completely risk free project. This means the project has to continuously identify and manage the potential problems the team may experience. Risk management is one of the essential tools that management has, next to leadership.

Formally defined, risk is the potential for the realization of unwanted negative consequences of an event (Dorofee et al). They can be risks associated with the project's schedule, the project's budget, or with the technical quality of the project's results. It is a potential problem that the V&V

team may experience. It may or may not happen, but it is advantageous for the V&V team to at least plan for it to happen as well as plan ways to avoid it happening. A risk has two attributes that you must manage. The first is the likelihood that the risk will become a realization. The second is the impact the risk will have if it does become a realization, called consequence. Figure 2.18 identifies these attributes and they are explained in more detail in Section 2.4.2.

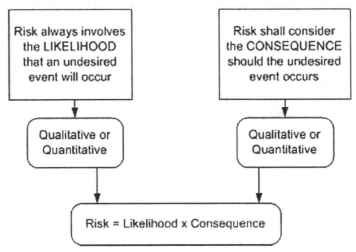

Fig. 2.18. Attributes of a Risk

Everyone on the project participates in risk management. All team members have a voice and it is essential that they all are heard. It is one of the basic principles often overlooked. Not including all team members or not listening to what they have to say is one of the common pitfalls experienced on projects today. This mentality breeds the "fire fighters" approach to performing V&V. The fire fighting approach refers to not doing anything until something goes wrong. In the past, the fire fighting mentality was accepted and even rewarded. How many projects have you been on when things went awry and management brought in outside people to save the day? Then they reward them! Completely foolish in my opinion and unfortunately it happens a lot. If only they would have listened and mitigated the potential problems the project would not have had to enter this crisis management mode. Now is the time for this to change and you as the leader can make this happen.

The good news is that we don't have to introduce new concepts. Risk management has been around for some time; the problem is that we have to actually implement it. Something that may not be as familiar is that on a V&V project, the V&V team can identify two kinds of risks. The first are risks associated with the V&V project (e.g. no team members have been trained on the new V&V method) and the second are risks associated with the development project (e.g. given that the software design has not been baselined and the project has begun implementation there is a concern that the source code will have to be drastically changed when the design is baselined). Risks against the development project are usually submitted to the developer's risk management system. Only in the event that the development team does not accept the V&V authored risk would the V&V team track it and resolve it.

Risk management incorporates a series of steps that are continuously performed during the life of the project to help the V&V team manage the uncertainty the future brings. Figure 2.19 identifies the series of steps that represent risk management.

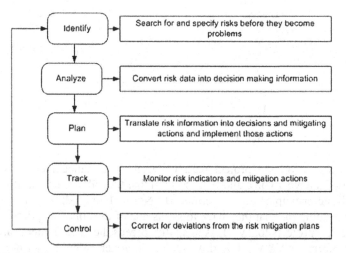

Fig. 2.19. Risk Management Steps

As stated before, risks associated with the development project normally go through the identify step and analyze step and then they are submitted to the developer's risk management system. So the remaining steps are not applicable to those kinds of risks, since the V&V team can not develop plans that the developers will execute.

Sections 2.4.1 through 2.4.5 introduce the sequence of steps by discussing its purpose, those responsible for the step, methods and tools for executing the step, the output of the step, and an example. Section 2.4.6 introduces the risk management plan and its contents.

Section 2.4.1 Identify

The identification step is a systematic attempt to specify the concerns to the V&V project as well as development project. The purpose of this step is to search for and specify risks before they become problems. All team members actively participate in this step and there are various methods and tools to help in the identification of risks. Table 2.8 lists some of them.

Table 2.8. Methods and Tools for the Identification of Risks

Method/Tool	Description
Brainstorming	All team members meet to discuss the potential problems the project may experience
Risk Item Checklist	Comprehensive checklists focused on general risks that may be applicable (e.g. budget risks, schedule risks)
Lessons Learned	Lessons learned database is analyzed for relevant past problems that may be experienced on the current project
Individual Uncertainties	Individual team members may have uncertainties about the project that must be considered and included.
Taxonomy-Based Questionnaire (TBQ)	Similar to a checklist except that TBQ attempts to identify risks by analyzing the answers to specific questions (e.g. are the V&V requirements stable? Answering this question No indicates that the V&V team is trying to hit a moving target and their success is at risk).
V&V Analysis	Analysis on the development artifacts may reveal specific issues but several of the same issue may indicate a risk or an issue that can not be proven with 100% certainty may be captured as a risk.

As an example, during the planning phase for a V&V project management decided to gather some of the team members together and conduct a brainstorming session regarding the potential problems they may face. One of the senior members on the team discusses a problem she has experienced on other V&V projects with the same development organization. The problem has to do with the fact that on the other V&V projects, the same developer had continuously slipped their schedule and delivered the software artifacts late. Management decided to capture this as a risk to the current V&V project since the V&V schedule was totally dependent on the developer's schedule.

The output of the identification step is a risk statement and risk description. The risk statement is structured and has two attributes, the first is the list of facts and the second is the consequence of those facts. (see Eq. 2.1)

Given that (list of facts) there is a concern that (consequence)   (2.1)

Using equation 2.1 and the example above, the risk statement would be; Given that the V&V schedule is totally dependent on the developer's delivery of software artifacts there is a concern that the V&V project will fall behind schedule if the development artifacts are delivered late.

The second output of this step is a risk description. The risk description provides additional detail regarding the risk. It may explain the facts in more detail or it may provide the analysis conducted that supports the risk. The description takes the place of the brevity contained in the risk statement and enables the next step to be conducted with better certainty.

Section 2.4.2 Analyze

The analysis step examines each risk in detail to determine the extent of the risks, how they relate to each other, and which ones are the most important. The purpose is to convert the risk data into decision making information.

During this step, the risk exposure is determined and the two attributes for risks are generated, the likelihood and consequence. (see Eq. 2.2) This will give a better understanding of the risk and supplies the necessary information for decisions to be made. Management is responsible for assuring that the step is performed but they will call on the subject matter experts to provide the values for the attributes. The values for the attributes can be qualitative or quantitative; in general it requires a subjective judgment to be made. Three methods are provided as an example in Table 2.9.

$$\text{Risk} = \text{Likelihood} * \text{Consequence} \qquad (2.2)$$

Table 2.9. Risk Analysis Methods

Method	Consequence	Likelihood
3-level	High	High
	Moderate	Moderate
	Low	Low
4-level	Catastrophic	Very high
	Critical	Likely
	Marginal	Not likely
	Negligible	Impossible
n-level	Project defined	Project defined

As stated before, assigning attribute values takes engineering judgment that is best performed by the team's subject matter experts. Table 2.10 provides some descriptions for the consequence attribute values for the 4-level method identified in Table 2.9. These descriptions differ from those normally documented simply because those that are somewhat standardized are relevant to development projects. The risks that we are concerned with are relevant to the V&V project. If the V&V team is authoring a risk against the development project then they will need to use the method employed by the development project.

Table 2.10. Consequence Descriptions

Consequence	Description
Catastrophic	Loss of human life, extensive damage to system, extensive slip to the critical path, extensive financial overrun or social loss, or complete failure to meet requirements.
Critical	Major or permanent injury, major damage to system, major slip to the critical path, major financial overrun or social loss, or major impact to requirements.
Marginal	Severe injury or illness, degradation of system, non-critical path tasks will overrun, some financial or social loss, or some requirements won't be met.
Negligible	Minor injury or illness, minor impact on system performance.

As an example, I will use the risk from section 2.4.1 which was:

Given that the V&V schedule is totally dependent on the developer's delivery of software artifacts there is a concern that the V&V project will fall behind schedule if the development artifacts are delivered late.

Using the descriptions from Table 2.10 I worked with the engineer that had raised this risk and we concluded that the consequence value was critical since there would be a major slip to the tasks on the critical path. It wouldn't have been an extensive slip because not all of the tasks that were affected by this risk were on the critical path. The likelihood that this risk would occur was scored as likely since every project our subject matter experts worked on the same developer was late in delivering the software artifacts. The reason it was not scored very high was that our experts had not worked on every project that the development organization was involved in, only those that had V&V projects. Our attributes for this risk then takes the form as shown in equation 2.3.

$$\text{Risk } 0001 = \text{likely} * \text{critical} \qquad (2.3)$$

The risk exposure is simply a way to categorize the risk with respect to the likelihood and consequence. You basically assign the risk to one of four categories, if you use the 4-level method. The four categories are determined at the start of the V&V project. An example is given in Table 2.11.

Table 2.11. Risk Exposure Table

	Very High	Likely	Not Likely	Impossible
Catastrophic	High	High	Moderate	Moderate
Critical	High	Moderate	Moderate	None
Marginal	Moderate	Moderate	Low	None
Negligible	Moderate	Low	Low	None

For our example risk, which was scored likely and critical (see Eq. 2.3), the risk exposure would be Moderate. So what does this all mean? Remember, the purpose of the analyze step is to convert risk data into decision making information. The decision making information that was generated are the attributes and the risk exposure. These will then serve, especially the risk exposure, the next step in the process, which is planning.

Section 2.4.3 Plan

The planning step is the process of deciding what, if anything should be done about a risk or set of related risks. It translates the risk information into decisions and mitigating actions and implements those actions. The project manager for the V&V team is responsible for the planning step, keeping in mind that team members may be assigned to take action on specific risks.

There are four possible actions that can be taken for a risk; research, accept, mitigate, and watch. Figure 2.20 presents a decision flow diagram to help identify which action should be taken.

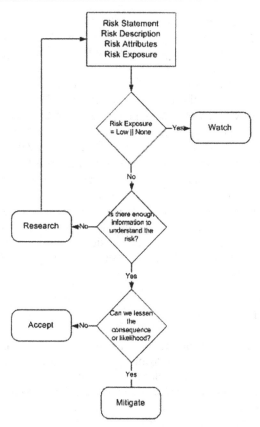

Fig. 2.20. Decision Flow for Assigning Risk Action

Regardless of the action taken, an action plan shall be established for each risk. If the action results in further research to be conducted then a research plan is established. If the action is to accept the risk then the acceptance rationale is documented as the action plan. If the action is to watch the risk then tracking requirements are documented as the action plan. Tracking requirements serve as triggering mechanisms in the event the risk changes or some other actions that serve to only monitor the risk in the event it changes. If the action is to mitigate the risk then a mitigation plan is developed and it serves as the action plan. The mitigation plan shall identify the actions to be taken, the due dates for the actions, those responsible for implementing the actions and the resources required.

For our example risk previously used, we would use the decision flow diagram to determine which action should be taken. There are two possible options, we could accept the risk since there really is nothing we can do to help the developers meet their schedule or we could mitigate the risk. I am of the opinion that for us to accept this risk would be the same as taking the fire fighting mentality, do nothing until the developers fall behind schedule.

I would choose to mitigate this risk. I would establish a mitigation plan that assigns actions to those responsible for establishing the communication channels between the developers and the V&V team. I would task them to proactively keep status on those development artifacts associated with the V&V tasks on the critical path. Using those status checks I would assign my subject matter experts with assessing whether or not our V&V team required the formal delivery of the development artifact or if a draft version could be used. It has been my experience that one main reason the developers have failed to deliver artifacts on time is because of the formalities associated with delivering final products. If our V&V team could achieve their objectives with a draft version of the artifacts and we could acquire them on time then we could avoid the latency experienced with delivery.

Section 2.4.4 Track

The tracking step is the process in which risk status data are acquired, compiled, and reported to the team as a whole. The purpose is to monitor the risk indicators, research plans and results and mitigation actions. It will also reassess the acceptance rationale to determine whether or not it is still valid. The project manager is responsible for this step as well as any team member assigned to the actions.

One method for implementing this step would be to conduct a monthly meeting where all risks are reviewed. Another approach would be to define the frequency of review based on the type of the action plan. If the action plan was to watch or accept the risk, then a monthly reassessment may be appropriate. If the action plan was to research the risk then once more information becomes available and a better understanding is obtained then a special meeting for the particular risk may be held. If the action plan was to mitigate the risk then once the actions defined in the mitigation plan are completed then the risk can be reassessed based on the results of the actions.

For our example above, the action was to mitigate. I would conduct monthly meetings that specifically addressed the particular risk. I would then use that meeting to assess whether or not the mitigation plan needs to be modified. Most of the time, the tracking step can be rolled up with the normal status meetings that management will hold on a V&V project. It is essential that if this step is rolled up into a standing management meeting that there is ample time allocated to reviewing risks.

Section 2.4.5 Control

The control step is the process that we have been leading up towards. All along we have been generating data to support the task of making informed decisions. The control step is just that, it is where the final decisions are made by taking the tracking status reports for the risks and deciding what to do with the risks based on the reported data.

Management has the primary responsibility but they will require feedback from all team members. During this step management will decide to close risks, develop contingency plans, modify action plans, or continue tracking and controlling.

It is essential that all information is communicated to all team members and the rationale for the decision made available. That is not to imply that management must have the entire team member's approval, it simply means that open communication is necessary to have a successful risk management strategy.

Section 2.4.6 Risk Management Plan

The Risk Management Plan documents the processes, approach, roles and responsibilities and rules of operation that will be followed on the V&V project. It can be integrated into the overall V&V project plan or stand alone. Regardless of its location, it shall at least contain the following:

- Overview
- Organization
- Risk Management Processes
- Communication
- Resources and Schedule
- Database for Risks

The overview section shall address the purpose and scope for the V&V risk management approach. It shall also identify all external references that have been used to develop the plan as well as those that may be used during the implementation of the plan. The last item of information that must be presented are the assumptions or constraints that have been used in developing the plan.

The organization section identifies the V&V project organization and those responsible for the risk management processes. Their roles must be defined and their relationship within the organization needs to be established. A key item of information that is often left out of the risk management plan is the identification of those that have the authority to make decisions. Make this very clear in the plan as well as during implementation.

The risk management processes section describes all the activities and how they are related. It describes the required procedures for each of the risk management steps and the methods to be used. It shall also describe any tools that will be used and the metrics collected that will enable the improvement of the risk management approach.

The communication section establishes how risks are to be reported among the team as well as externally. Reporting formats are established and frequency of communication is scheduled.

The resources and schedule section shall identify when the risk management activities are carried out. In addition, this is where the amount of resources is identified that is required for the implementation of the plan.

One of the last items that have to be included in the plan is the location and the use of the risk management tool that will be used to maintain and manage the list of risks identified. There are numerous tools that exist today, from the normal spreadsheet models to online databases. I would advocate the use of the more robust online databases. These tend to be more structured and centered on a formal process. Using a spreadsheet enables shortcuts to be taken as well as risks to be deleted. In this day of advanced technology, obtaining a tool devoted to risk management is not difficult.

Section 2.5 Communication Structures

This section of the book discusses communication strategies and organizational structures that the V&V project may assume. Communication during the life of the V&V project is essential. Not only is it essential to communicate amongst the team it is essential that all stakeholders receive the information they need for the success of the V&V project. The way the V&V team is organized will influence the communication paths that are established. There are three basic organizational models for a V&V team:

- Embedded
- Internal

- Independent

An embedded V&V team is one in which the team members are also members of the development organization. They are a component of the development team. The V&V engineers basically have two responsibilities. Their first responsibility is to that of the development team and they must fullfill their engineering duties. Their second responsibility is to that of the V&V team. Normally the development engineers spend some ratio of work hours devoted to their seperate responsibilities (e.g. 70% development and 30% V&V). The project manager for the software development project normally serves as the V&V project manager as well. Figure 2.21 shows an embedded V&V team and the flow of information.

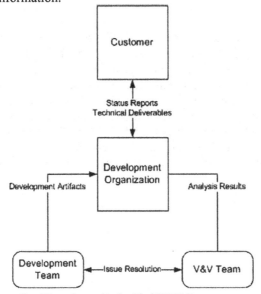

Fig. 2.21. Information Flow for an Embedded V&V Team

An embedded V&V team has one informal communication channel and it is between the V&V team members and their colleagues on the development team. V&V engineers perform analysis on development artifacts that they have not engineered themselves and provide results to the team in general and try to resolve any issues within the development team. Their communication with the customer is normally rolled up within the status reports and formal reviews conducted during the development life-cycle.

An embedded V&V team is commonly found on smaller projects with smaller project budgets. The following rules must be followed to have a successful embedded V&V team:

- The development engineers and V&V engineers must work flawlessly as a team. This means they have to be acceptable to the issues raised and have the willingness to do the right thing.
- The V&V engineers must be steadfast to not perform V&V on the engineering artifacts they develop.
- The V&V engineers must have a willingness to thoroughly analyze their colleague's work.
- The project manager can not be schedule and cost driven. Their limited resources demand a solid issue tracking system and risk management approach.

An internal V&V team is depicted in Figure 2.22. This organization has a dedicated quality assurance group that may have its own resources, which the V&V engineers would not have to serve on the development team. Informal issue resolution takes place between the V&V engineers and the development engineers. Resolution of all issues is attempted at the lowest level before they are raised higher. Formal issue resolution would then take place between the heads of the organizations for those issues that can not be resolved at the development level. There is still one communication channell between the development organization and the customer.

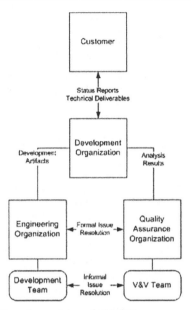

Fig. 2.22. Information Flow for an Internal V&V Team

Some advantages and disadvantages to this type of model are:

- Since the V&V engineers are not part of the development team they devote all of their time to the assurance of the system software.
- Since the V&V engineers are not part of the development team it can create difficult working relations between the two teams. Serious attention has to be given to establishing and maintaining good communication between the developers and V&V'ers.
- It is advantageous for the V&V team to do whatever they can to resolve their issues directly with the development team. Once the V&V team raises issues to the organization level then the communication channel will be adversely affected.

An independent V&V (IV&V) team is depicted in Figure 2.23. Under this model there are two separate organizations that communicate with the customer. The first organization is the development organization. The second organization is the quality assurance organization hired directly by the customer. The V&V team attempts to resolve any issues at the lowest level. In the event that issues cannot be resolved at the lowest level then issues can be raised and worked all the way up to the customer. Analysis reports generated by the V&V team are delivered directly to the customer as well as status reports regarding the V&V project.

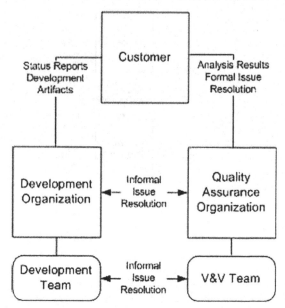

Fig. 2.23. Information Flow for an Independent V&V Team

The IV&V team has all the benefits of being totally separate from the development organization. They have their own budget, their own management, and their existence is not dependent on the success of the development project. With these benefits come challenges. The biggest challenge for the IV&V team is establishing good communication with the development team. It would benefit the project manager of the V&V team to expend a great amount of effort in assuring that communication is open and working effectively.

Depending on which organization structure your V&V team chooses, the V&V project manager must identify all stakeholders and the information they require. There are two major sources of information, issues and analysis results. You must identify where each type of information is to flow as well as to whom. This is depicted in an information flow diagram and maintained in the Project Plan. This information flow diagram represents what information is generated by the V&V team and where that information goes.

References

Chillarege, Ram (1996) Chapter 9: Orthogonal Defect Classification, Handbook of Software Reliability Engineering, McGraw Hill

Dorofee, Audrey, Julie Walker, Christopher Alberts, Ronald Higuera, Richard Murphy, Ray Williams (1996) Continuous Risk Management Guidebook. Carnegie Mellon University

Fagan, M.E (1976) Design and Code Inspections to Reduce Errors in Program Development, IBM Systems Journal., vol. 15, No. 3

Minford, John (2002) The Art Of War by Sun-tzu. New York: Viking Penguin

Chapter 3: The Verification and Validation Life Cycle

The Verification and Validation (V&V) life-cycle is easily understood if you are familiar with a traditional software engineering life cycle. A generic model of the V&V life-cycle is depicted in Figure 3.1. The intent of the figure is to put the V&V life-cycle in perspective with a traditional software engineering life-cycle.

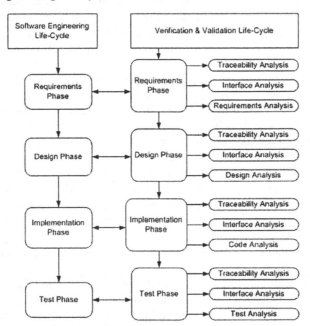

Fig. 3.1. Verification and Validation (V&V) life-cycle model in relation with a traditional software engineering life-cycle. For example, the V&V requirements phase is in-line with the software engineering requirements phase in which the V&V team fulfills the requirements of traceability analysis, interface analysis, and requirements analysis.

The software engineer reading this book is going to flail up their arms in disgust that I left out a few phases in the software engineering life-cycle. Your systems engineer is going to quickly try to relate this generic model to the newly defined "V-Model". Your V&V professionals are squirming in their chairs wondering about the maintenance activities they perform analysis on as well as the operational aspects of V&V. To all I reply, at least you are paying attention. On a serious note, the intent of this book is to discuss the core activities that V&V performs. V&V can perform several other types of assessments on a wide range of artifacts; this book is focusing on those that make up the foundation for a V&V project. In the life-cycle, V&V performs requirements analysis when the development project is engineering their requirements. V&V performs design analysis when the development project is engineering their designs, and so on. As you quickly see in the figure, traceability analysis and interface analysis is executed at the beginning of each phase. That is not a coincidence, it was designed that way. We'll discuss this more when we discuss traceability and interface analysis. For those not familiar with the traditional software engineering life-cycle then let me take a moment to put things in perspective.

Development projects typically assume a traditional phased-approach to engineering their system. They define their requirements, they architect a solution in the format of a design. They implement the design using code and then they test their implementation. This life-cycle can be generically characterized as having four basic phases; requirements phase, design phase, implementation phase, and test phase. Literature, academia, and practice may choose to use different terms but they are more than likely very similar to what was just described. The V&V project in turn will execute in phases and their phases run in parallel, or in phase, with the development project. When development is generating requirements then the V&V project is performing requirements analysis. This life-cycle, when coupled with the V&V requirements, makes up the foundation for the V&V project.

If you recall the requirements and scope discussions in Chapter 2, V&V has a set of high-level requirements that they must fulfill. In addition to the requirements, they have also defined their scope of work, which translates to the parts of the system that V&V must perform their work on. The requirements and scope are represented in Figure 3.2. This 50,000 foot view depicts what needs to be achieved by the V&V project as well as what parts of the system requires scrutiny.

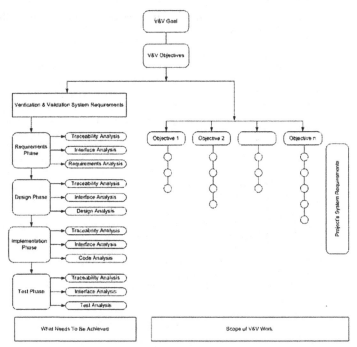

Fig. 3.2. Overview of V&V life-cycle, V&V requirements, and V&V scope. The goal of V&V is the root node, objectives are established to meet the goal, and requirements and the scope of work are established to meet the objectives and goal.

The requirements represented on the left side of the figure will be further refined for each phase of the life-cycle. As an example, you'll see more when you read the rest of this chapter, during each phase the V&V team refines the system-level V&V requirements for the particular phase. This refinement is depicted in Figure 3.3. As you can see in the figure, the V&V team starts with the high-level V&V system requirements and for each particular phase they refine the requirements such that they are applicable for the phase in which V&V is functioning. The example shows the refinement during the requirements phase and the refinement is a simple qualification of parent and child elements. During the requirements phase, child elements become software requirements and parent elements become system requirements. This simple refinement led to the development of the 15 standard V&V system requirements. If one was to study each phase and each requirement you would see that the only difference between phases is that you work on different artifacts. The V&V team wants to fulfill the same requirements for each phase but they are specific for which artifacts they are working on (i.e. during requirements phase V&V is concerned with requirements, during design they are concerned with the elements that make up the design).

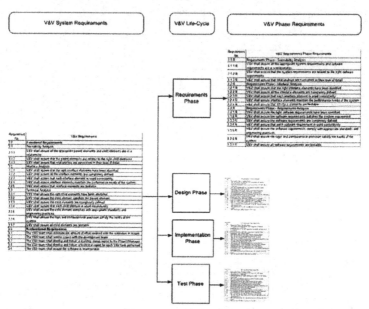

Fig. 3.3. The refinement of V&V system requirements to V&V life-cycle phase. The V&V project starts with their V&V System Requirements and refines them for each phase in the V&V life-cycle.

The specific requirements that get derived during each phase are introduced in their appropriate sections. Section 3.1 discusses traceability analysis and section 3.2 presents interface analysis. These are presented in their entirety in their own section, even though they are performed during each phase, because their differences across phases are minimal. Section 3.3 presents the technical analyses that are performed during the life-cycle phases. Specifically, section 3.3.1 discusses requirements analysis, section 3.3.2 discusses design analysis, section 3.3.3 discusses code analysis, and section 3.3.4 discusses test analysis.

Section 3.4 introduces the concepts of software testing from a V&V perspective. For each type of analysis (e.g. requirements analysis, design analysis, etcetera) one of the discussion threads has to deal with the various approaches that engineers and scientists can take to perform the analysis. The approaches are categorized as being manual analysis, static analysis, dynamic analysis, or formal analysis. The main reason for the classification is simply for organizational purposes. A side benefit to classification includes better planning and estimations. The concept of V&V testing can be categorized as dynamic analysis. The V&V team executes the artifact under scrutiny (i.e. execute a model representing the requirements) in order to derive the behavioral aspects of the system. The V&V team can use these behavioral aspects to fulfill some of the requirements levied upon them. The reason that V&V testing has a section all to itself is because testing is a very large subject that is applicable to all of the phases, not just one particular phase.

Section 3.1 Traceability Analysis

The foundation for the V&V effort exists in the relationships between originating requirements and their resulting system features. These relationships are an enabler of future V&V tasks. They act like roads on a map that associate software features to the system requirements within scope of V&V. They permit the verification and validation of properties set forth in the concept and system requirements to assure they have been carried forward to the software specification, software design, implemented in the code, included in the test plan and test cases, and provided to the customer and user in the resulting system.

Traceability is established in all the life-cycle phases and V&V's traceability analysis requirements are refined based on the life-cycle phase in which they are executed. For example during the requirements phase, traceability analysis focuses on system requirements and software requirements. During the design phase, traceability analysis focuses on software requirements and elements of the design. During the analysis, the preceding phase is considered the parent and the current phase is considered the child. So during requirements phase, the parents are the system requirements and the children are the software requirements. Figure 3.4 identifies the domain for traceability analysis during the life-cycle phases.

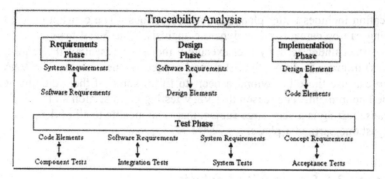

Fig. 3.4. The domain space for the life-cycle phases during traceability analysis. During the requirements phase the domain space consists of system requirements and software requirements. During the design phase the domain space consists of the software requirements and design elements.

Traceability analysis requirements are then refined using the domain space depicted in Figure 3.4. Tables 3.1, 3.2, 3.3, and 3.4 present the traceability analysis requirements as they pertain to the life-cycle phase. The first column in each table represents the requirement number. The number is appended with a character from the set of {R, D, I, T}. Each letter represents the phase in which the requirement is applicable. For example, an 'R' represents requirements applicable to the requirements phase (see Table 3.1). A character 'D' represents requirements applicable to the design phase (see Table 3.2). A character 'I' represents requirements applicable to the implementation phase (see Table 3.3), and the character 'T' represents requirements applicable to the test phase (see Table 3.4). The character is appended to the requirement number strictly for reasons for discussions in this book. To make referencing easier I added the character to the requirement number, something that may not need to be done in practice.

Table 3.1. Traceability analysis requirements for the Requirements Phase

Requirement No.	V&V Requirement
3.1.1.R	V&V shall assure all the appropriate system requirents and software requirements are in a relationship.
3.1.2.R	V&V shall assure that the system requirements are related to the right software requirements.
3.1.3.R	V&V shall assure that relationships are consistent in their level of detail.

Table 3.2. Traceability analysis requirements for the Design Phase

Requirement No.	V&V Requirement
3.1.1.D	V&V shall assure all the appropriate software requirements and design elements are in a relationship.
3.1.2.D	V&V shall assure that the software requirements are related to the right design elements.
3.1.3.D	V&V shall assure that relationships are consistent in their level of detail.

Table 3.3. Traceability analysis requirements for the Implementation Phase

Requirement No.	V&V Requirement
3.1.1.I	V&V shall assure all the appropriate design elements and code elements are in a relationship.
3.1.2.I	V&V shall assure that the design elements are related to the right code elements.
3.1.3.I	V&V shall assure that relationships are consistent in their level of detail.

Table 3.4. Traceability analysis requirements for the Test Phase

Requirement No.	V&V Requirement
3.1.1.T	V&V shall assure all the appropriate code elements and component tests are in a relationship.
3.1.2.T	V&V shall assure all the appropriate software requirements and integration tests are in a relationship.
3.1.3.T	V&V shall assure all the appropriate system requirements and system tests are in a relationship.
3.1.4.T	V&V shall assure all the appropriate concept requirements and acceptance tests are in a relationship.
3.1.5.T	V&V shall assure that the code elements are related to the right component tests.
3.1.6.T	V&V shall assure that the software requirements are related to the right integration tests.
3.1.7.T	V&V shall assure that the system requirements are related to

	the right system tests.
3.1.8.T	V&V shall assure that the concept requirements are related to the right acceptance tests.
3.1.9.T	V&V shall assure that relationships are consistent in their level of detail.

These requirements are used to define what V&V needs to achieve with respect to traceability. Just as you saw in the planning section of Chapter 2, these requirements drive the tasks that V&V must perform. To fulfill all of these traceability analysis requirements, V&V has to perform two high-level tasks; first they must establish the relationships and second they have to assess them. Assessing the resultant relationships fulfills the V&V traceability analysis requirements. The first task of establishing relationships involves developing links between parent elements and child elements. This means that relationships have to be established between:

- System requirements and software requirements, and vice versa
- Software requirements and design elements, and vice versa
- Design elements and code elements, and vice versa
- Code elements and component tests, and vice versa
- Software requirements and integration tests, and vice versa
- Sytem requirements and systems tests, and vice versa
- Concept requirements and acceptance tests, and vice versa.

The V&V team has an option in performing this first task. If the development team has already established the trace between elements within and between artifacts then the V&V team can elect to bypass this step or press forward and develop their own. Normally the artifact that is used to represent traceability relationships is called a traceability matrix.

For the V&V team to establish a traceability matrix on their own is currently a manual process. Analysts need to become familiar with the system requirements that are within scope and then study the software requirements to determine which ones are related to the system requirements. This of course is during the requirements phase. If the analysts were performing the trace during the coding phase then the analysts would become familiar with the design elements (e.g. modules) within scope and then study the code to determine which code elements (e.g. functions) are related to the design modules. The development of the traceability relationships by the V&V team is very time consuming and dependent on the domain experience of the analyst. For example, the analyst may be concerned with the stored commanding system functionality. She would then study the software requirements and possibly identify software functionality related to certain events that cause a sequence of commands to be executed. She would then establish a relationship between the two.

This approach would be considered manual analysis. Static analysis pushes the envelope a great deal with the use of natural language processing, where software tools parse the artifacts under scrutiny and match requirements together based on the domain represented in the requirements. Similar domains are an indicator of being related. There is great promise in this technique which would certainly yield faster times for the derivation of traceability relationships.

It seems advantageous at this point in time for the V&V team to assume the traceability established by the development team and assess it. However, there is a lot to be said for V&V teams that generate their own relationships and compare them with the developers.

However the V&V Team wishes to implement this first task, either use the traceability established by the development team or by the V&V team, the relationships (between parent and child elements and child and parent elements) are then assessed to fulfill the traceability requirements identified in the above tables.

During the requirements phase, the tasks that need to be performed by the V&V team, to fulfill the traceability requirements, are:

- Determine if all the applicable system requirements are associated with at least one software requirement.
- Determine if all of the software requirements are associated with at least one system requriement.
- Determine if all the applicable system requirements are associated with the right software requirements and vice-versa.
- Determine if the level of detail within the relationships is consistent for all of the requirements within scope.

These tasks, when achieved, will fulfill the traceability analysis requirements represented in Table 3.1. So let's walk through these tasks to make sure we have the same level of understanding as to what V&V is doing for traceability analysis. First I'll discuss these tasks and then I'll follow up with an example with the intent to clarify any ambiguous words that may appear in their descriptions.

The first two tasks listed above satisfy requirement 3.1.1.R in Table 3.1, which was *"V&V shall assure all the appropriate system requirements and software requirements are in a relationship."* The first task is basically checking that all the software-related system requirements, that are within scope, are linked to some software requirement. This is providing assurance that the system feature of interest has been allocated to the software and not left out. The second task is doing the same thing but only establishing the backward relationship. It is concentrating on the software requirements that are within scope and making sure that they are related to at least one system requirement. This is to assure that there are no hidden software features being developed. A common term for this is "Easter Eggs" and can be found in numerous software packages, which take the form as "back doors" into the system without the customer knowing that they were built in.

A manual approach is taken to perform these two tasks. It does not require much effort, as long as the traceability matrix is easily understood. It consists of doing a quick-check to make sure that everything within scope is linked to something. Don't read any more into this, this is all that is done to fulfill this traceability analysis requirement. If the development team is using software tools to aid them in engineering the requirements then this becomes a very rapid check, push button if you will.

The third task in the above list *"Determine if all the applicable system requirements are associated with the right software requirements and vice-versa"* satisfies requirement 3.1.2.R in Table 3.1. This task is a little more involved than the first two mentioned but not by much. It is assessing the relationships as to whether they are the right relationships. With respect to traceability and the relationships established between the system requirements and software requirements, the focus of this criterion is only on the relationships. Meaning, is the relationship between System requirement 1.1.2 and software requirement 4.1 the right relationship? This is not to be confused with requirements analysis, which addresses whether or not the software requirement satisfies the system requirement. This is not requirements analysis it is traceability analysis, your only concern is whether or not the system requirement is traced to the right software requirement. The software requirement may not be correct but if it is addressing the functionality and domain represented in the system requirement then traceability analysis would pass this relationship. Requirements analysis would reveal whether the requirement was correct or not.

Whether you are analyzing the relationships between system requirements to software requirements, software requirements to design elements, design elements to source code elements, or source code elements to test cases the task remains the same. Simply answer the question "is this the right relationship?"

The approach taken to perform this task is normally a manual approach. It involves an analyst studying the system requirements to identify the domain of the requirement. The domain of the requirement can be extracted by simply answering the question "What is the requirement talking about?"

So if you were given the following requirement:

"Requirement 3.4.3.2 MUGSEY 0x01 shall receive commands from the ground and process them within 10 seconds."

The analyst may determine that the domain of the requirement is a set of commands. The analyst would then look at which software requirement, or requirements, this system requirement was linked with to determine what the domain is of the software requirement(s). If the above system requirement was linked to the following software requirement:

"Requirement OS 2.4.6.2 Command Processing shall receive, depacket, and process real-time commands sent from the ground."

The analyst may determine that the domain for this requirement is a set of real-time commands. Now the analyst just needs to compare the domains and determine if they are talking about the same thing. More formally, the analyst has to determine whether the software requirement's domain is a subset of the system requirement. This approach is what is normally performed. Sometimes, analysts will use additional attributes to assess the relationship. I advocate these additional attributes for the sole reason that to truly fulfill the traceability analysis requirement other criterion need to be assessed.

In addition to the domain, the action that the requirement performs as well as when the action is to be performed should be compared. Table 3.5 is a data structure that can be used to extract the attributes from the requirements being assessed. You can populate this table for the system requirements being assessed and then develop a table for the software requirements being assessed. Then the tables can be compared to each other to determine if the system requirements are linked to the right software requirements.

Table 3.5. Data structure for determining whether or not the system requirement is traced to the right software requirement

Requirement Number	Requirement Title	Domain	Action	When to take Action
3.4.3.2	Real-time Commanding	Commands	Receive	When sent from Ground
3.4.3.2	Real-time Commanding	Commands	Process	Within 10 seconds of receipt

The fourth task in the above list, *"Determine if the level of detail within the relationships is consistent for all of the elements within scope"*, satisfies requirement 3.1.3.R in Table 3.1. Determining the level of detail that is represented in the relationship is manual in nature and involves engineering judgment. Science can help out in this arena to lessen the amount of subjectivity. The results of fulfilling this requirement are used to determine the level of maturity for the artifacts being assessed. To meet this requirement, the analyst has to first identify the level of detail that exists in the relationships. Once the level of detail is determined the analyst needs to determine if there is a consistent level of detail being used for all the relationships in the system. Figure 3.5 is one way to represent the level of detail within relationships.

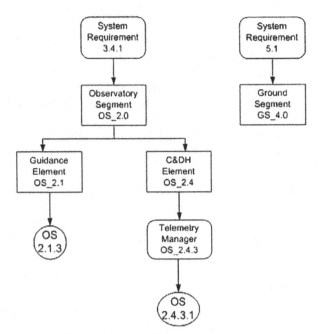

Fig. 3.5. Level of detail for the relationships representing the two system requirements

This figure can be used to determine if there is a consistent level of detail being represented by the relationships in the system. In this example, you can quickly see that system requirement 3.4.1 is linked to a third-level software requirement and a fourth-level software requirement, OS 2.1.3 and OS 2.4.3.1 respectively. These lower-level software requirements even refine the system requirement by providing more detail. On the other hand, system requirement 5.1 is linked to software requirements that make up the ground segment (GS_4.0). Comparing these two links you can easily see that the level of detail that makes up the relationships is not consistent between the two. The latter simply allocates all of the ground segment requirements to the system requirement while the former calls out the specific software requirements. The one thing to note here is that as a result of this consistency check, issues are not normally generated based on consistent use of the same level of detail. For example, in Figure 3.5, even though there is not a consistent level of detail being used I would not author an issue. The reason is based on the engineering judgment used to do the consistency check. It isn't readily clear that there is a real problem here; there is a concern but not necessarily a problem. I would author a risk at the Project level. A risk that calls out the fact the ground segment has yet to mature enough so that system requirements can be allocated to it. Having said that, there probably would be an issue generated from one of the other tasks since there is a lack of ground requirements. However, just because the project is not consistent with the level of detail does not immediately cause a problem but it does cause a concern.

At the completion of these four tasks, the V&V team has established a strong foundation for its future activities as well as provided insight to the development effort as to the maturity of the software requirements. The results of executing these tasks provide the development project with the following assurance:

- The system requirements of concern have been allocated to the software.
- There are no additional software requirements allocated to the system.
- The system requriements of concern are linked to the right software requirements.
- The level of detail used within the relationships is consistent for the system requirements of concern.

Now that we have a description of the tasks that are needed to be exe-cuted to fulfill the traceability analysis requirements, let's use an example to clear up any questions. Take for example the traceability matrix pro-vided by the development organization to the V&V team regarding Project MUGSEY 0x01(See Table 3.6). The first and second columns identify the system requirements and the third and fourth columns identify the software requirements that are related to the system requirement (e.g. System Re-quirement 3.4.1 is related to Software Requirements OS 2.1.3 and OS 2.4.3.1). The traceability matrix represents those system requirements that came out of the scoping exercise discussed in Chapter 2. These are the system requirements of concern to the V&V effort. Specifically, these are the system requirements associated with the third V&V objective *"Provide assurance that the system software can reliably communicate with the ground."* For our example, the V&V team is performing traceability analysis on these system requirements associated with communicating with the ground segment.

Table 3.6. Traceability Matrix provided by the MUGSEY 0x01 development team

System Reqt. No.	System Requirement	Software Reqt. No.	Software Requirement
3.4.1	MUGSEY shall telemeter the position of the vehicle during ascent and descent to the ground segment.	OS 2.1.3	The Guidance Element shall packetize the altitude and position data along with the local time and send this packet to the Memory Manager and to the Telemetry Manager of the C&DH Element.
		OS 2.4.3.1	Telemetry Manager shall send the position of the Observatory Element, to the ground, once every 10 seconds.
3.4.2	MUGSEY 0x01 shall provide a connection to allow for data recovery.	OS 2.4.2.3	Memory manager shall provide an interface to downlink the data after recovery.
3.4.3.2	MUGSEY 0x01 shall receive commands from the ground and process them within 10 seconds.	OS 2.4.6.2	Command Processing shall receive, depacket, and process real-time commands sent from the ground.
4.1	MUGSEY 0x01 shall separate the observatory segment from the launch segment when commanded or when it reaches 50,000 feet in altitude.	OS 2.4.5.2	If the observatory detects that it has achieved an altitude of 50,000 feet it shall issue a separate command to the Recovery Segment.
		RS 3.2	The recovery segment shall separate the observatory segment from the launch segment when commanded.
5.1	MUGSEY 0x01 shall be able to receive all telemetry during ascent and descent.	Ground	
5.2	MUGSEY 0x01 operations shall send commands during ascent and descent from the ground operations.	Ground	

To fulfill the traceability analysis requirements we have to perform four tasks:

- Task 1: Determine if all the system requirements are associated with at least one software requirement.
- Task 2: Determine if all of the software requirements are associated with at least one system requriement.
- Task 3: Determine if all the system requirements are associated with the right software requirements and vice-versa.
- Task 4: Determine if the level of detail within the relationships is consistent for all of the requirements within scope.

Task one is perfomed by looking at the traceability matrix and determining if all of the system requirements are at least linked to one software requirement. We would write one V&V issue against the last entries in the table, system requirements 5.1 and 5.2, which are linked to the ground and do not have any requirements defined. For the time being we will label this first issue VV_Issue_R0001.

Task two is performed similarly by looking at all of the software requirements and assuring that they are linked to at least one system requirement. To perform this task we choose to build the data structures identified in Table 3.5. Figure 3.6 is the data structure for the system requirements and Figure 3.7 represents the software requirements.

System Requirement	Domain	Action	When to take action
3.4.1	position of vehicle	telemeter	during ascent and descent
3.4.2	data	provide	connected to ground
3.4.3.2	commands	receive	when sent from ground
	commands	process	within 10 seconds of receipt
4.1	commands	separate	when sent from ground
	altitude	separate	when it reaches 50K feet
5.1	telemetry	receive	during ascent and descent
5.2	commands	send	during ascent and descent

Fig. 3.6. Traceability data used for assessing system requirements

Software Requirement	Domain	Action	When to take action
OS 2.1.3	position data and local time	packetize	?
	packet	send	?
OS 2.4.3.1	position of Observatory Element	send	every 10 seconds
OS 2.4.2.3	data	provide	after recovery
OS 2.4.6.2	real-time commands	receive, depacket, and proc	when sent from ground
OS 2.4.5.2	command	issue	when altitude = 50K feet
RS 3.2	commands	separate	when commanded
Ground			
Ground			

Fig. 3.7. Traceability data used for assessing software requirements

Using these two figures we can determine whether or not there are additional software requirements that are not linked to a system need. There are a few areas of concern. First, software requirement OS 2.1.3, which is linked to system requirement 3.4.1 identifies functionality for building packets of data that will contain the position of the vehicle as well as the local time. There are no system requirements for building packets of data. This software requirement, even though the development team has linked it to system requirement 3.4.1 does not seem to have a related system requirement. Even though this may be an oversight at the system level, I would still author a V&V issue about this. I would write an issue because the software developers are going to develop the software such that it bundles all of the data into packets and then sends those packets to the ground. The systems engineers have not identified that as being needed or they have overlooked it and missed some system requirements. I would author a second V&V issue labeled VV_Issue_R0002 detailing this discrepancy.

The second area of concern is with software requirement OS 2.4.2.3, which is linked to system requirement 3.4.2. The system requirement indicates it wants a hard connection to the vehicle in order to retrieve data. The software requirement provides that but indicates that it will be used "after recovery" (see the column titled "When to take action" in Figure 3.7). The frequency for retrieving data does not seem to be consistent; however this is not a problem for traceability analysis to solve. This will get resolved when we perform requirements analysis. So at this time I would only flag it so that the V&V team does not forget to follow up.

The third task to be performed by V&V is to determine whether the relationships established are the right relationships. We use Figures 3.6 and 3.7 to aid us in the assessment. The concern here is again with software requirement OS 2.1.3 and system requirement 3.4.1. The software is adding functionality that there does not seem to be a system need for (see the action column in Figure 3.7). The software indicates that there will be some protocol to which the data is bundled together and system requirement 3.4.1 does not state that is a need. Software requirement OS 2.4.6.2 reinforces this concern by stating that it will receive, depacket, and process real-time commands. Depacketing the commands suggests the ground will bundle the commands together with other data, although there are no system requirements to support this. These concerns would be added to VV_Issue_R0002 for resolution.

Another concern that would definitely have an issue authored against it would be with the relationship between system requirement 3.4.3.2 and software requirement OS 2.4.6.2. The system requirement states that commands are to be processed within 10 seconds. The software requirement, which it is linked to, does not carry the timing constraint forward. As such, the system requirement is not linked to the right software requirement. Actually, after looking for the right software requirement that it should be linked with I could not find one. As a result I would author an issue, VV_Issue_R0003, for the identification of the right software requirement for system requirement 3.4.3.2.

The last concern has to deal with the fact that there are no requirements identified for the ground segment, yet there are system requirements allocated to it. I would add this data to the first issue, VV_Issue_R0001, for resolution.

The last task deals with determining whether there is a consistent level of detail represented in the traceability matrix. I built the graph presented in Figure 3.8 to represent the level of information that is depicted in the traceability matrix. The root nodes represent the system requirements, labeled as such, and the circles represent the software requirements. Starting at one of the system requirements you can trace down through the structure of the software requirements to see which software requirement the system feature is specifically linked.

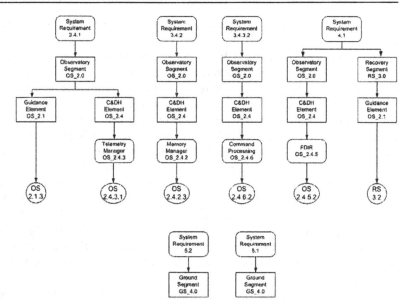

Fig. 3.8. Graph representing the level of information represented in the traceability matrix

In looking at the graph you can see that four of the six system requirements have a structured graph beneath them revealing the level of detail that represents the trace. Two of the six, system requirements 5.2 and 5.1 do not have any depth to their trace. What does all this mean? Well first there are only two areas that skip a level of information. System requirements 3.4.1 and 4.1 have branches that skip one of the levels of information. This is not a concern since they are separate sections of the software requirements and do not adhere to the same structuring. The last thing that this shows is exactly what our already written issues have stated, and that is the ground segment of the software is not mature enough to provide the level of detail needed to establish a trace. It is also indicative that V&V won't be able to fulfill their other assessments simply because the information does not exist. This concern would generate a V&V risk because it impacts future V&V tasks and needs to be managed.

So what are the V&V results and what has V&V provided development. The V&V objective that we were focusing on for this example was for V&V to provide assurance that the system software can reliably communicate with the ground. This identified the system requirements of interest to the V&V team. Next the V&V team needed to fulfill their traceability analysis requirements by performing four tasks. The results of those tasks can be summarized at the requirements level and reported back to the project.

The first requirement that V&V needed to fulfill was to provide assurance that the system requirements have been allocated to the software, for those system requirements that represent communicating with the ground. There is one issue that V&V is reporting and that deals with the fact that the ground segment has yet to have their requirements defined. As such, not all of the system requirements can be shown to have been allocated to the software. The second part of the first requirement that V&V needed to fulfill was to provide assurance that all of the software requirements can be related to a system need, for those software requirements associated with communicating with the ground. There is one issue that V&V is reporting and that deals with the software providing a capability to packet data that is collected during operations. There is not a system requirement that calls for this functionality. In addition there is a concern that the software will depacket the commands sent to it from the ground and yet the ground has not indicated that it will follow such a protocol.

The second requirement that V&V needed to fulfill was to provide assurance that the system requirements are related to the right software requirements, for those system requirements that represent communicating with the ground. There is one concern that V&V is reporting and that deals with the fact that there is a system requirement that is not linked to the right software requirement. The system requirement deals with processing commands within 10 seconds but the software requirement associated with this does not carry the timing constraint forward.

The last requirement that V&V needed to fulfill was to provide assurance that the relationships were consistent in their level of detail. The concern that V&V had was that there were no ground segment requirements defined for their associated system requirements. Although this is a concern, V&V is not writing an issue for this concern since the first issue already covers this area.

Lastly, V&V is opening a V&V risk that it will manage itself. The risk has to do with the fact that given the ground segment requirements have yet to be defined there is a concern that V&V will not be able to meet their objectives and schedule. The V&V team will manage this risk and mitigate it by resolving the issues that have been opened.

All of the V&V tasks performed to meet their traceability analysis requirements were performed manually. This is a concern of the author simply because it would not be difficult to build tools to help analysts in performing these tasks. Static analysis would benefit from the use of tools that parse system requirements and software requirements to extract the data needed to populate something like that depicted in Table 3.5. Tools that use the same requirements documents as well as the traceability matrix could build graphs that depict the level of information represented by the traceability matrix. These tools would not replace the engineers but it would certainly speed up the execution. One last note that I want to discuss is something that science could solve for the engineering community. This has to deal with defining "levels of detail" as well as what it means to be consistent in its use. Are there any correlations between the levels of detail and issues? This is something that science could provide and then tools could be built to take it one step further.

To fulfill the traceability analysis requirements within the other life-cycle phases is a simple translation of the tasks already defined. For example, during the implementation phase, the remaining tasks that need to be performed to fulfill the requirements of traceability analysis (see Table 3.3) are:

- Determine if all the applicable design elements are associated with at least one code element.
- Determine if all of the code elements are associated with at least one design element.
- Determine if all the applicable design elements are associated with the right code elements and vice-versa.
- Determine if the level of detail within the relationships is consistent for all of the elements within scope.

As you can see all you have to do is simply place the artifacts of interest into the task description. If you are in the design phase then substitute child elements with design elements and substitute the parent element with software requriement. The tasking is the same except for which it is applied and that is dependent on the artifacts that are under scrutiny.

The last thread of discussion that I want to cover has to do with the various V&V approaches and how science can advance the engineering practice. In the past it has largely been a manual effort in fulfilling the traceability analysis requirements, however there are a few areas that look promising.

Science needs to focus on providing support in the automatic generation of traceability matrices. Even if science did provide this capability to the engineering community it wouldn't alleviate the need to perform traceability analysis. You would still have the engineer in the loop, but it wouldn't be so resource intensive. One area in need of advancement is natural language processing, which could prove beneficial in establishing traceability matrices.

Other areas that science could provide valuable support include visualization techniques to aid in the assessment of traceability matrices. The examples I have used in this book have been smaller sets of larger traceability matrices. So visually scanning them in search of requirements not associated with anything has been quite easy. Projects that have a significant number of requirements, somewhere in the order of 500 requirements, the visual assessment that engineers perform breaks down. Visual techniques would also yield great rewards in communicating back to the development project the results of traceability analysis.

Tools to support the extraction of the domain and functionality of requirements would improve the engineering assessments focused on determining whether or not the parent element is linked to the right child element. To date, it requires the engineer to identify the action the requirement wants performed as well as the domain in which the action is applicable. Tools to help the identification of these requirement's attributes would speed up the process as well as keep the engineers from missing something in the large data that is accumulated.

The last area that provides fertile ground for science is the exploration of what it means to have a consistent level of detail. What does it truly mean to not be consistent, is it a problem? This last area, which is largely a subjective assessment by a V&V analyst, would see great return if science could provide some support.

Section 3.2 Interface Analysis

Any time information has to be moved from one item to another (one module to another, one procedure to another) there is always a chance that it can be corrupted or used the wrong way. Systems engineers find it advantageous to modularize their designs, as they should. This allows for different teams to build the individual modules. Keep in mind it is not only done so that we can use different teams, it is beneficial because you break the problem down into smaller more manageable parts. It then becomes the job of the systems engineer to plug these modules together in order to have a complete system. The individual teams would normally build their modules according to some specification that dictates how they are to communicate with the other modules (e.g. an Interface Control Document (ICD)). Some engineering projects even have working engineering models that the teams can use to test their modules prior to integration. Even though this approach is favored there are a variety of problems that can occur (e.g. engineering models aren't accurate, software implementation truncates data values). As such, the V&V team focuses their effort during each life-cycle phase on the elements that enable the communication between software modules.

For each of the life-cycle phases the V&V team wants to make sure that the right interface elements have been identified, are completely defined, are used consistently, maintain the performance needs of the system, and can be verified via testing. These requirements are to be fulfilled for each phase. Traceability analysis has established what parts of the system that V&V is concerned with. It is the responsibility of interface analysis to now make sure they are right. The specific requirements that V&V must fulfill are stated in Table 3.7. The one noticeable difference, as compared to the traceability analysis requirements, is that there is only one set of interface analysis requirements for all of the life-cycle phases. For the interface analysis requirements, there is no need to interchange the wording based on the phase in which you are in. The requirements are the same for all of the phases.

Table 3.7. Interface Analysis requirements for the various life-cycle phases.

Requirement No.	V&V Requirement
3.2.1	V&V shall assure that the right interface elements have been identified.
3.2.2	V&V shall assure all the interface elements are completely defined.
3.2.3	V&V shall assure that each interface element is used consistently.
3.2.4	V&V shall assure interface elements maintain the performance needs of the system.
3.2.5	V&V shall assure that interface elements are testable.

For the V&V team to fulfill their interface analysis requirements identified in Table 3.7, they need to perform the following generic tasks.

- Task 1: Identify the data that should be past between modules.
- Task 2: Identify the interfaces that should handle the data transactions.
- Task 3: Compare the V&V defined interfaces with those defined by the developers and assess the inconsistencies.
- Task 4: Analyze each data item and determine if it is completely defined.
- Task 5: Graph the locations where the data items are used and determine if they are used consistently.
- Task 6: Identify the performance needs of the system.

- Task 7: Model and simulate the communication between interfaces to determine if these performance needs are maintained.
- Task 8: Develop tests for the interfaces and identify which ones are not testable.

Tasks one and two are setting the stage for the validation effort. It is the up-front work that V&V needs to perform to assess whether or not the developers have identified the right interfaces. These are very expensive tasks to perform and require subject matter experts (SMEs). It would be advantageous for a V&V organization to either use or begin building an oracle of knowledge that encapsulates best practices for defining interfaces. In executing these tasks, your V&V analysts act as if they were the developers responsible for engineering the interfaces in order to define what data needs to be communicated through the system as well as the interfaces responsible for managing the communication. Use cases and scenarios (e.g. sequence diagrams) are an excellent tool for the V&V analysts to capture what they feel the system should have along the lines of data and interfaces. Data flow diagrams are another good tool that I have used extensively. It is at this point that V&V is defining what data they feel needs to be passed through the system. There are a handful of ways in which the V&V team can approach this, they can perform a brainstorming session where they try to hack out all of the data that might be needed, they can study similar systems and extract the data that they communicate, or they could prototype the system and see what data they need to have communicated through the system. These approaches are dependent on one thing and that is the objectives that the V&V team are trying to achieve. The reason I feel it is dependent on the objectives is that if the V&V team's objective was focused on the identification and handling of faults then they may use fault trees or Failure Modes to help identify the data that is needed to be communicated.

Task three is dependent on the results of task one and two. Once the data and interfaces are defined by the V&V analysts they can compare this to what the developers have actually engineered. Again, this is a manual process for the V&V analysts to compare what they think should exist to what actually does exist. This is the validation step, where the V&V effort is assuring that the right interface elements have been identified. Take note that this does not have to be a manual process. There has been promising return from V&V teams that have modeled the developer's interfaces and executed them to derive their apparent behavior. V&V analysts can then assess this behavior to what they thought should have been revealed. Also note that this can be done with the requirements, design, code and even the tests. The corner stone for fulfilling the first interface analysis requirement, *"V&V shall assure that the right interface elements have been identified"*, lies in the results of tasks one, two, and three. In order to determine whether or not the development team has identified the right interfaces requires the V&V team to compare them against something. That something is developed during the execution of task one and two.

Task four requires each data item, identified during Task 1, to be assessed for completeness. Completeness checklists can and should be developed to define what it means for a data item to be complete. To begin with, an organization may choose to use the following list. The V&V analyst needs to assure the following items of information are provided for each data item:

- The units of measure the data represents
- The required precision for the data
- The range of values the data may take on
- The timing in which the data needs to be processed
- The source of data
- The destination of data

If temperature readings are being passed between modules and the ICD defines temperature as the data item then the V&V team will assure that the ICD has also identified what measurement system that temperature is being represented in (e.g. Celsius). The V&V team will also check to make sure the required precision is defined and the minimum and maximum values that the temperature may be recorded in. They also need to check if there are timing requirements for which temperature readings have to be pushed through the system. Lastly, the source of the data item and its destination shall be identified and represented for each data item. Completeness checks should be represented in some knowledge base so that the task can be repeated.

Task five involves mapping all the usages of each data item. Once the analysts know where all the data items are being used they can assess whether or not those items are being used consistently. When performing interface analysis on code there are numerous tools to support this. This would be considered static analysis, since the SME uses a tool to aid them in their assessment. Any dependency browsing tool reveals all of the locations of data items. It becomes more and more manual as the development teams use natural languages (e.g. English language) to represent the engineering artifacts. When the development teams incorporate the use of tools then the process becomes more static and possibly dynamic. There has also been a breakthrough in the dynamic analysis approach especially when interfaces are used to provide control of the system. These specifications are modeled (e.g. using tabular notation as in the Software Cost Reduction (SCR) tool) and then simulated to assure consistent use of data items and state transitions (Heitmeyer et al 1998). Even though this approach has been marketed as a requirements analysis approach it can be beneficial during the requirements phase when you have interface requirements to assess.

Task six and seven are pretty vague activities and hard to define generically. The problem that the V&V team is trying to solve is whether or not the interfaces maintain the performance needs of the system. So if the system requires commands to be processed within 10 seconds of receipt then the V&V team needs to assure that the interfaces defined can achieve this performance. This is a very clear example for why V&V is a systems engineering discipline. In order to assess whether or not the interfaces can maintain the performance requirement of processing commands within 10 seconds of receipt requires the V&V team to take into consideration the entire thread of execution from receiving the signal, recognizing the command, handling an interrupt, routing the command to the appropriate terminal and giving the terminal processing time. My point is simply this, as a V&V analyst you have to take into consideration everything that can affect that timing requirement.

One approach an analyst can take is to actually test these performance needs. However, the V&V effort would not provide any direct benefit to the requirements and design phases if they waited on the code to be written to actually test the interfaces. There are other dynamic analysis approaches that can be used but it requires modeling the interfaces and then simulating them. This is an immature area for V&V, which is surprising since modeling and simulation is not an immature discipline to the engineering community. The reason that I say it is immature from a V&V perspective is that we can not do it cheaply. To date, there are no slick methods that allow us to quickly model the interfaces, using the requirements, and then simulate them. It also requires a lot of configuration management effort since you have to assure that your models maintain the integrity of the requirements as they change. Another problem that V&V has to guard against is if an issue surfaces then they have to ensure that it wasn't their model that generated the issue and that it actually was the developed interfaces.

Task eight is pretty straight forward and requires all the interfaces of concern to V&V to be pre-tested. Pre-tested in this sense means the V&V team needs to develop tests for the interfaces of interest and flag those that can not be tested. In developing tests the V&V team is concerned with whether or not the interfaces can be verified via execution.

These tasks which I have just discussed can be further explained via an example. I will again call upon project MUGSEY 0x01 for demonstration. During the requirements phase one of the V&V objectives is to provide assurance that the software interfaces adequately support the identification and handling of faults. The system requirements of interest to V&V because of this objective are identified in Table 3.8. In Table 3.8 the first and second columns identify the system requirements and the third and fourth columns identify the software requirements that are related. For example, system requirement 3.4.3.1 is related to software requirement OS 2.4.5.1.

Table 3.8. System requirements of interest to V&V during interface analysis.

System Reqt. Number	System Requirement	Software Reqt. Number	Software Requirement
3.4.3.1	Stored Commanding	OS 2.4.5.1	FDIR
6.3	Fault Handling	OS 2.1.6	Guidance Element – Update
		OS 2.1.7	Guidance Element - Invalidate
6.3.1	Science Faults	OS 2.4.2.1	Memory Manager
		OS 2.4.4	Watchdog Timer
6.3.2	Abort Mission	OS 2.4.5.1	FDIR

System requirement 3.4.3.1, stored commanding, states *"MUGSEY 0x01 shall process a command sequence upon entering a failure scenario."* It has been allocated to the Fault Detection Isolation and Recovery (FDIR) software requirements. The specific software requirement to which it associated is OS 2.4.5.1, which states *"If the observatory detects a descent rate of (TBD) feet per second it shall dispatch a RECOVERY command sequence."* We will use this as our example and step through the tasks identified above.

Task one and two, again, are the precursor to the validation effort and require the V&V team to identify what data and interfaces need to be defined for the system and user needs. In order to identify the data items that need to be passed between modules requires the V&V team to identify a set of potential faults that the system could experience. The second task will then require the V&V team to identify the interfaces needed to identify and handle these potential faults. This data will be used during the remaining V&V tasks because the V&V team needs to fulfill their requirements to meet their objective. The V&V team came up with the following set of potential faults.

- Global Positioning System (GPS) stops sending position data and the system is not aware that is has stopped so it keeps using the last reading from GPS.
- Temperature sensors stop sending temperature readings and the system is not aware that it has stopped so it keeps using the last known readings form the temperature sensors.
- Guidance element stops sending position data but it does update the watchdog timer so the system is not aware that the guidance element has stopped.
- Altitude decreases or remains the same due to winds on the vehicle and the system thinks it is descending.
- Observatory fails to recognize when it is descending.

Using this small set of potential faults, which the team developed during a brainstorming session, the V&V team then developed a data flow diagram to represent the data that should be passed in order to identify or handle these faults. Figure 3.9 is the data flow diagram used to represent the first fault, when GPS stops sending data but the system is unaware that it has stopped so it keeps using the last reading. The data flow diagram only encapsulates what the V&V team thought should be communicated with respect to the two requirements identified above (System requirement 3.4.3.1 and software requirement OS 2.4.5.1). Data flow diagrams would need to be built for the remaining requirements from Table 3.8.

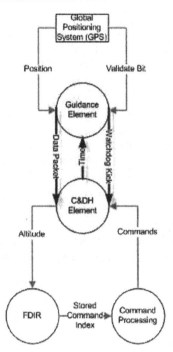

Fig. 3.9. Example data flow diagram used during interface analysis. This data flow represents what data the V&V team thinks should be represented in the system to handle a fault with the GPS unit.

Task 3 is then performed to compare what the V&V team felt should be defined against what the development team did define. In Figure 3.9 the V&V team felt that a GPS unit would provide position data as well as a validation bit to the Guidance Element. The validation bit would be used to indicate whether or not the GPS unit is responding. The logic would be very similar to a watchdog timer in that the GPS updates the bit every so many seconds to let the system know that it is operating nominally. If the validation bit is not sent then the system would know that it has invalid data and would not use it. The V&V team also expects the Fault Detection Isolation and Recovery (FDIR) subsystem to receive altitude data across the interface and in response send an index to the command processing subsystem. The index that is sent across the interface would be a reference value for a specific sequence of commands to be executed. The specific sequence of commands would be identified by command processing using the value of the index. There are 5 data items of interest to V&V in this example which are captured in Table 3.9.

Table 3.9. Data items of interest during interface analysis. The data items were generated by assessing a potential fault in which GPS would stop sending data but the system was unaware that it had failed. These data items are what the V&V team feels should be represented to at least be able to identify and handle the fault.

Data Item	Sent From	Sent Where
Position	GPS	Guidance Element
Validate Bit	GPS	Guidance Element
Altitude	C&DH Element	FDIR
Stored Command Index	FDIR	Command Processing
Commands	Command Processing	C&DH Element

The V&V team would then use this information to compare against the developer's defined interfaces. A snapshot of the developer's requirements, data-flow diagram, is depicted in Figure 3.10. In looking at the figure you can see that the developers have not included GPS sending a *validate bit*, or anything like it, to the Guidance Element.

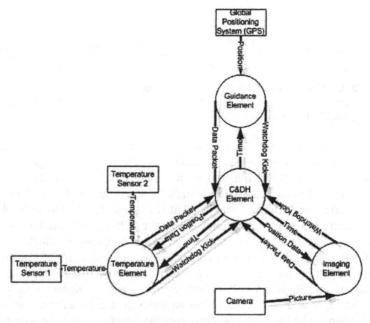

Fig. 3.10. The developer's data flow diagram used to compare against the interfaces that the V&V team developed. The inconsistencies are assessed to determine if the developers have identified the right interface elements.

The data flow diagram does not have to specifically identify a "validate bit" but what the V&V team was looking for was some data item to be passed between GPS and the Guidance element that would indicate whether data was stale or not. Too many times we have encountered problems of reading from registers that aren't zeroed after a reading and the source does not update the register with new data but the destination module keeps reading from the register thinking the data is new. This is a concern to the V&V team since data from GPS could become old if GPS fails. In bringing this concern up to the developers they had agreed with our concern. However, they could not modify the information sent from GPS, since they are buying it off the shelf. Instead they are adding a requirement to the Guidance Element to make sure that it is receiving valid data from GPS.

The other concern that comes out of tasks one, two, and three has to do with the specificity of software requirement OS 2.4.5.1. I know, you've probably not heard that before, since when is it a problem to be too specific? The problem that the V&V team has is that the project has only specified one sequence of commands to be dispatched for all possible failure scenarios (see Figure 3.11). As such, their FDIR only sends one mnemonic for all possible failures and the V&V team does not believe that the system should respond to all possible failures with a RECOVERY command sequence. According to the master command database, the RECOVERY command sequence turns on the strobe, beeper and then separates the observatory from the balloon. This means that if the temperature sensors stop sending temperature readings then the observatory will separate from the balloon and end the mission prematurely. The V&V team feels that an index into a table of commands should be sent from FDIR to the command processor so that the development team would have different options for dealing with different failure scenarios.

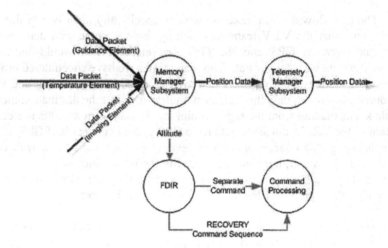

Fig. 3.11. Data flow diagram for the C&DH subsystems responsible for responding to failures. In the figure you can see that only one command sequence, RECOVERY, is sent in the event of a failure.

As the V&V team wraps up tasks one, two, and three they are left with interfaces that they feel should exist to meet the needs of the system. These interfaces may not be complete but at least the V&V team is comfortable with the fact that all the elements that are needed have been identified. Now the V&V team performs task 4 to determine if the data items are completely defined. As stated before, a checklist is a great starting point for the V&V team. Our V&V team will check to make sure the following items are defined for each data item in Table 3.9:

- The units of measure the data represents
- The required precision for the data
- The range of values the data may take on
- The timing in which the data needs to be processed
- Source of data
- Destination of data

Please note that the data items in Table 3.9 are for only one particular fault and the V&V team would have to look at all data items that were identified from tasks one and two. This task is also dependent on the format in which the data items are being represented. If the developers are using tools to define their interfaces or data dictionary then the V&V team can automate the completeness check. Tools are beginning to be used pretty frequently in which some tools require the designer to identify all of the data items attributes the first time an item is introduced into the system.

In the event that developers have not evolved to using tools then this can become another manual process for the V&V team. You are probably seeing a trend in which it would seem advantageous for the V&V team to perform one initial task at the beginning of each phase which would be entering the developer's data into some common framework for V&V tools to operate in. It may be effort-intensive at first but I believe it would pay off in the long run.

The V&V team has made sure that all of the appropriate interface elements are present and completely defined. Now task 5 is performed to assure that wherever those elements are used in the system they are used in a similar fashion as they were previously defined. This is where a dependency browser is extremely important. If the developers are only writing their requirements in a text document then this task becomes an extremely manual process for the V&V team during the requirements phase. Using the example above, the V&V team would search for all occurrences of the data item *altitude* and make sure that it is being used as it was defined in task four. Meaning, task four may have revealed that *altitude* readings will be maintained with a precision of 5 digits and have a range of 0 to 99000. However, the V&V team may see in the developer's interface requirements that *altitude* readings will maintain *altitude* using 2 decimal values which can make *altitude* values 7 digits (e.g. 39987.23). This is not consistent with its original definition. The design should indicate some base B with a precision of p to show how the values should be kept. Although it may not be a problem it needs to be investigated, especially the affects that the change of precision has on the accuracy of the values.

The next series of tasks that V&V must perform to fulfill interface analysis requirement 3.2.4 deal with extracting the performance needs of the system and assessing the interfaces to assure that they can meet those performance constraints. These tasks, task 6 and 7, can become a very specialized assessment and resource intensive. If you are in the requirements and design phases then the V&V team must take a modeling and possibly a simulation approach. If the software has been developed then static analysis can be used or the software can be executed to extract the performance behaviors.

Let's tackle the latter problem because I feel that performing this task during the implementation phase or beyond is more mature than the former. The V&V team has several approaches that they can take. They can use a logic analyzer to measure the execution time of each module. One advantage is that this approach will take into account hardware latencies as well as other delays that occur that sometimes are missed when focusing solely on instruction execution times. The major drawback is that the

V&V team has to have hardware in the loop, which means they will need to schedule time in the developer's labs to perform the assessment.

Another approach that can be taken is to count the instructions and sum their execution times. Again this approach requires the source code and it needs to be assembled. Once you have the assembly code then the loading time can be computed for the cycle. Take each instruction and label it with its execution time (e.g. floating point instructions normally take 40 micro-seconds to execute), take the longest path possible through the code and add the execution times.

One last approach that can be used is to instrument the code, calling the systems clock, and measuring the times of execution for transmission across the interfaces. Again, this requires executing the code and emulating the hardware. It also presents another problem to the V&V team in that the instrumented code now has to take into consideration the newly inserted instructions. If they are not cleverly placed then they can create issues that are not normally experienced with the original code.

The previous paragraphs dealt with the software already implemented and available to the V&V team. What can we do if we are in the requirements phase? Well we can model the requirements and analyze the times, providing best guesses when needed, for transmissions across the interfaces and determine if this will meet the needs of the system. Sequence diagrams and timing diagrams are very useful tools for performing this analysis. Timing diagrams have been used for a very long time especially by electrical engineers. A timing diagram is simply a graph with time along the horizontal axis and the possible states of the software along the vertical axis. Figure 3.12 shows an example timing diagram.

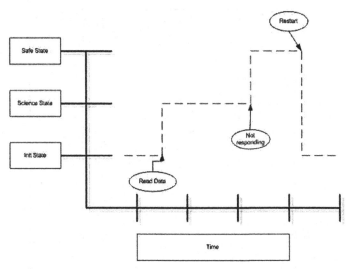

Fig. 3.12. Example timing diagram where time is represented on the horizontal axis and the possible software states are represented on the vertical axis. The events that trigger a transition between states is represented in the bubbles. The vertical axis could also be used to represent tasks or modules.

Sequence diagrams are also very useful to represent the communication between modules. They can be instrumented with time, algorithms, notes, and etcetera. Both timing diagrams and sequence diagrams do require tool support to be completely effective. You can create these diagrams using any graphical editor but to actually perform the analysis requires the tools to understand the semantics of the objects that make up the diagram so that you can execute them. Figure 3.13 is an example sequence diagram.

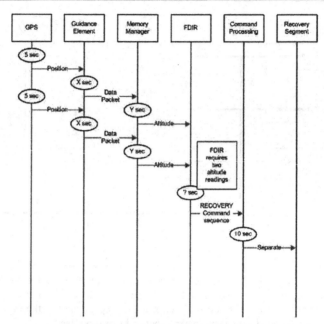

Fig. 3.13. An example sequence diagram for project MUGSEY 0x01. It depicts the interactions and messages sent between modules if a fault was to occur during operations. The real time extensions to modeling (e.g. Unified Modeling Language) now enable the V&V groups to assess requirements and designs using simple notations.

When you have the software architecture defined then you can incorporate some architectural design language to help model the architecture and simulate the execution times. Again this is dependent on the format in which the developers provide their artifacts and the resources that V&V are willing to spend. These modeling and simulation approaches, dynamic approaches, are very expensive for V&V to perform.

The last task that V&V must perform is to determine whether or not the interface elements can be verified via testing. Section 3.4 goes into great depth regarding testing, which all of the principles apply here. Even though I refer you to that section I will add a few notes here. The one thing to take away from this section is that to meet the interface analysis requirement does not require the V&V team to actually test the interfaces. What you have to do is determine if they are testable. The best way to do that is to simply develop tests for the data items which will indirectly show you which ones are not testable. The dependency browser that you used previously comes in useful in executing this task. It not only shows you which data items are of interest it shows you where they need to be tested, which you can derive tests to execute those sections. For example, our objective for assuring that the system can identify and handle faults identified one interface and data item of interest to be GPS communicating the position data item with the guidance element. The V&V team needs to determine whether or not GPS and the guidance element can be tested.

In summary the V&V team fulfilled its interface analysis requirements and provided insight into the quality of the interfaces by answering the following questions.

1) Do the developers have the right interfaces defined?
2) Are those interfaces completely described?
3) Are those interfaces used consistently throughout the system?
4) Do those interfaces maintain the performance needs of the system?
5) Are those interfaces able to be verified by testing?

Section 3.3 Phase Dependent Analysis

The purpose of the following sections is not to describe every possible tool or approach available for performing V&V. The intent of the remaining sections is to identify exactly what needs to be achieved when doing V&V. I expect this knowledge to be used when selecting the appropriate tools or methods for performing the V&V work. There are so many different techniques that can be used when performing V&V. For example, when doing code analysis a lot of the time people think of it as running the code through a static analyzer to look for faults. Believe me, this is not V&V. It is a part of V&V but it is not complete. I feel what needs to be first understood are the requirements that V&V must meet and then tools and methods can be selected based on their coverage on those requirements.

The phase-dependent analyses can be generically referred to as technical analysis. The V&V requirements are actually the same for each phase of the life-cycle. This sounds unbelievable but it's true! During each of the phases; requirements phase, design phase, implementation phase, and test phase the V&V requirements are all the same. They are depicted in Table 3.10. Just as we saw in traceability analysis the only difference does not lie in the requirements it lies in the domain in which the requirements are applied. So for example, during requirements analysis, child elements are replaced with software requirements and parent elements are replaced with system requirements. For each phase you simply change the name of the element according to the phase in which you are in.

Table 3.10. Technical requirements that V&V must fulfill for each phase of the development life-cycle.

Requirement No.	V&V Requirement
3.3.1	V&V shall assure the right child elements have been identified.
3.3.2	V&V shall assure the child elements satisfy the parent elements.
3.3.3	V&V shall assure the child elements are completely defined.
3.3.4	V&V shall assure that each child element is used consistently.
3.3.5	V&V shall assure the child elements comply with appropriate standards and engineering practices.
3.3.6	V&V shall assure the logic and computational precision satisfy the needs of the system.
3.3.7	V&V shall assure all child elements are testable.

The core foundation from which V&V shall establish their results lies in the structure of the requirements. Take a hard look at the requirements and you'll see a simple transition. First V&V makes sure that the right things are identified (i.e. the right requirements have been established). Then V&V makes sure they satisfy their parent elements (i.e. the software requirement satisfies the system requirement). Then V&V makes sure they are completely defined. Then V&V makes sure they are used consistently. Then V&V makes sure they comply with best practices. Then V&V assures the performance constraints are met and lastly V&V makes sure they can be tested. This simple transition is not to be overlooked. It has been built in to the requirements so that V&V never has to do rework without a major change being performed by the project. For example, if V&V first made sure that requirements were used consistently and then they made sure the project had defined the right requirements then any missing requirements would cause V&V to go back and assess consistency again. I guess you can say that these temporal properties could be achieved via scheduling the tasks appropriately, well that is true but instead I wanted to build it into the requirements.

As I stated before, the requirements are the same for each phase of the life-cycle. For each phase you simply change the name of the element according to the phase in which you are in. In the remaining sections the requirements are qualified for their particular phase. After the requirements are refined for the particular phase I discuss any differences in approaches that should be taken during that particular phase. You'll see that the approaches too are very similar across the phases and their main difference lies in the format in which the artifacts are presented to the V&V team. For example, during the requirements phase the V&V team will have to assure the right software requirements have been identified. More than likely, as input they will work on a text document with the requirements written in the English language. During implementation phase the V&V team will have to assure the right code elements have been identified. More than likely, as input they will work on a flat file with source code written in a particular programming language. The requirements that V&V shall meet are the same. The difference is that during the requirements phase they will achieve the requirement on a text document and during the implementation phase they will achieve the requirement on a .cpp file. Figure 3.14 depicts the approach that I recommend taking when performing V&V. The recommendation moves away from conducting V&V manually towards a more dynamic approach in which modeling and simulation is incorporated. The intent is not to remove the domain experts from performing V&V; the intent is to arm them with better resources.

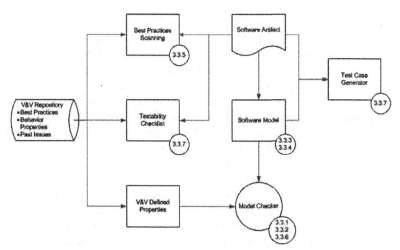

Fig. 3.14. Recommended approach for performing V&V. The circles with numbers in them represent the V&V requirement that is met by performing the certain V&V task.

Let me summarize the approach that I am recommending. For all the phases the V&V team is going to get some kind of artifact that represents the system during that phase (e.g. software requirements specification). Taking a dynamic analysis approach requires the V&V team to model the system at the given phase, which means the team is going to have to develop a model using the software artifacts provided. V&V will then have to define the properties that they feel the system should exhibit. Together, these properties and the model of the software are fed into a model checker that explores whether or not those properties hold. Just in doing these tasks the V&V team will have fulfilled five of the seven requirements. In fulfilling the requirements they assured the right elements have been defined, they satisfy their parent elements, they are completely defined and used consistently and the performance needs of the system are maintained with the current set of software elements. The last two requirements that need fulfilled are assuring the software elements comply with standards and best practices and assuring the software elements are testable. For the former I recommend a static analysis approach in which tools are employed to automatically scan the artifacts and flag areas of interest for the domain expert to further explore. The latter requirement also needs tool support however this support comes in the form of automatic test case generation.

All in all this approach is surprisingly not that drastic of a change in how V&V is currently done. You'll see a variety of approaches. Some V&V projects simply bring in good people and have them manually review documents. Other V&V projects not only adopt the approach described above but in addition bring in the scientists to actually prove, mathematically, that certain properties hold in the given system. Which approach is the right one, that's the million dollar question. The reason that I recommend the approach above is twofold. First it is feasible, the technology exists and it is sound and has been proven. Second, it compliments the developer's approach. This approach provides an additional level of rigor that is not performed on the project simply because of budget and schedule constraints. This is something that a V&V project can bring to the development project that is unique and scientifically sound.

Section 3.3.1 presents requirements analysis and the requirements that V&V must meet during that phase. Section 3.3.2 introduces design analysis, section 3.3.3 introduces code analysis, and section 3.3.4 introduces test analysis. For each section I identify exactly what needs to be achieved from the analysis and then discuss the various approaches that should be taken to perform V&V. The various approaches are organized based on whether they are manual analysis, static analysis, dynamic analysis, or formal analysis.

Section 3.3.1 Requirements Analysis

Requirements analysis is conducted by the V&V team to provide assurance that the right software requirements have been identified, they satisfy the needs of the system, they are consistent, and they can be verified by testing. It is during the requirements phase that the development project will establish what the software system is supposed to do. This phase of the life cycle is the most critical and V&V can have the biggest impact by fulfilling the V&V requirements for this phase. I firmly believe that if I ever get "extra" money to perform V&V I would apply it to the requirements analysis phase. This has the biggest return for both the V&V effort as well as the development effort.

The requirements that the V&V team must fulfill are identified in Table 3.11. These requirements drive the selection of tasks as well as the approaches that V&V can take. There are various approaches that V&V can take to fulfill these requirements. From manually reviewing requirement specifications, performing static analysis on the documents, modeling and executing the specification and mathematically proving the existence or omission of specific properties. During this phase of the life cycle the V&V team has already established the system features of interest for the V&V effort and they have confirmed that they have been allocated to the software through traceability analysis. The V&V team has also assured that interface requirements are adequate to support the needs of the system. Now is the time to determine the technical merit of the software requirements. As you can see in Table 3.11, the requirements that V&V must fulfill are an essential measure to the development group regarding the quality of their requirements.

Table 3.11. V&V requirements that shall be fulfilled by the V&V effort during requirements analysis.

Requirement No.	V&V Requirement
3.3.1.R	V&V shall assure the right software requirements have been identified.
3.3.2.R	V&V shall assure the software requirements satisfy the system requirement.
3.3.3.R	V&V shall assure the software requirements are completely defined.
3.3.4.R	V&V shall assure that each software requirement is used consistently.
3.3.5.R	V&V shall assure the software requirements comply with appropriate standards and engineering practices.
3.3.6.R	V&V shall assure the logic and computational precision satisfy the needs of the system.
3.3.7.R	V&V shall assure all software requirements are testable.

As stated in the introduction I am not prepared, nor is anybody, to discuss every available tool that exists on the market or in the research labs for conducting requirements analysis. However, I will discuss what these requirements mean and what needs to be achieved by the V&V effort for requirements analysis. This can then be used to identify the tools and methods that the V&V team needs to use.

There are four approaches that the V&V team can take, each with different resource requirements and each having a different outcome. The four approaches are manual analysis, static analysis, dynamic analysis, and formal analysis. During the planning phase the V&V team has to be diligent in planning for which approaches are going to be used for each analysis being performed. This is not something to be decided upon later in the project. Let me say that again, this is not to be decided upon later it has to be planned for in the beginning. You'll see why when we discuss the approaches.

Manual analysis is simply a domain expert that is brought in to review the software requirements. She relies solely on her experience and knowledge. She studies the artifacts under scrutiny and she makes observations that are based on that experience and knowledge. This is an expensive approach to take because domain experts are not cheap. The other disadvantage to taking this approach is that you don't have a clear understanding on whether the domain expert, through studying the requirements, met the V&V requirements for this phase. The other disadvantage is that it would be difficult to repeat the analysis and achieve the same results using different analysts. For example, let's say I was brought it to perform requirements analysis and I need to fulfill the requirements identified in Table 3.11.

The problem that I am trying to answer in fulfilling the first requirement is if the project has identified the right software requirements. A manual approach limits the options that I have to solve this problem. I can brainstorm before studying their software requirements and develop my own requirements, data flow diagrams, or use cases. I can study an oracle that has captured functionality from previous projects that are related to this domain. I can study a similar project from the past to understand the functionality that they defined and use this as part of my knowledge base. No matter what I choose it is completely reliant on what I can think of, it's as if I am the developer and I need to identify the requirements that I feel should be present. Once I have defined them I will then compare that to what the developers have come up with. This validation step is totally dependent on being able to compare what is being built to something that states what should be built. I can't advocate enough the need for an oracle of knowledge that captures what has been built in the past so that we can use it for our validation tasks on future projects. As an example, I would expect an organization that does V&V to have requirements for a Watchdog Timer in some oracle so that I can use during my validation tasks.

The problem I am trying to answer in fulfilling the second requirement is whether or not the defined software requirements satisfy the system requirements. Manually this can be almost impossible. Simply because it comes down to a gut feeling as to whether the software requirement can meet the needs of the system. Analytical approaches are sometimes limited with the complexity of requirements, especially if the requirements are written in the English language. As an example, we have a software requirement that states that it needs to scrub memory and correct single bit upsets and detect multiple bit upsets every 5 seconds. It is suppose to be satisfying the system requirement that needs no failure in the system to keep science readings from being taken for longer than 5 minutes. This is a difficult job for an analyst to determine whether scrubbing memory every 5 seconds is adequate to meet the needs of the system. They would have to take into consideration the radiation environment that will be experienced during operations, the hardware specifications regarding their material, the load on the processor when scrubbing is taking place, the run-time of the scrubbing algorithm, etcetera. Analytically this is a very resource intensive job, it is possible to solve but extremely time consuming. Before everyone starts arguing with me that they could solve that problem analytically I'll concede now. I wanted to get your attention. The main point is that just manually reviewing the document is not going to completely fulfill the V&V requirements for this phase.

The third problem that I need to solve to fulfill the third requirement is to determine whether or not the software requirements are completely defined. There are various interpretations for the word complete and how that applies to requirements. First, we could solve this problem by manually reviewing the software requirements against a standard checklist. For example, have they defined the units of measure for all values represented in the requirement, have they identified the input and the output for the function being described as well as the source of the input? Have they identified the accuracy needed in the measure that they are taking? These types of checklists can be covered by a manual review. However, I think that these checklists do not cover another aspect to what the V&V requirement is demanding. For a requirement or requirement set to be complete the functionality that the requirement is describing has to be complete. So if there are different states that the particular requirement is associated with then are all the states and how they transition defined? This is difficult to determine manually and you'll see in later paragraphs that there are methods that exist to help in doing this so there is no reason to do this manually.

I am going to leave the manual analysis discussion and jump right into how I think V&V should approach fulfilling their requirements. The reason is this, the technology exists and we should be using it. Not to replace the analyst but to help them do their job even better than they have done it in the past. I recommend that the approaches in Table 3.12 be used when performing requirements analysis.

Table 3.12. Recommended approaches to fulfilling the V&V requirements during requirements analysis

Requirement No.	V&V Requirement	V&V Approach
3.3.1.R	V&V shall assure the right software requirements have been identified.	Dynamic Analysis and Formal Analysis
3.3.2.R	V&V shall assure the software requirements satisfy the system requirement.	Dynamic Analysis and Formal Analysis
3.3.3.R	V&V shall assure the software requirements are completely defined.	Manual Analysis and Static Analysis
3.3.4.R	V&V shall assure that each software requirement is used consistently.	Static Analysis
3.3.5.R	V&V shall assure the software requirements comply with appropriate standards and engineering practices.	Static Analysis
3.3.6.R	V&V shall assure the logic and computational precision satisfy the needs of the system.	Dynamic Analysis
3.3.7.R	V&V shall assure all software requirements are testable.	Static Analysis

Dynamic and formal analysis is precisely where V&V should be in performing requirements validation. I simply chose both approaches because it is difficult to distinguish between the two sometimes. For example, if I model my requirements using the SCR tool set I am taking a formal approach to modeling the requirements. However, one of the benefits of using this methodology and tool set is that it has a simulation capability that will allow you to execute the model, a dynamic analysis approach. Instead of trying to differentiate between the two I chose not to waste the energy. The simulation capability has the ability to identify the differences between what the V&V analysts perceive the requirements to be and the behavior captured in the software requirements. The model in Figure 3.15 is

the recommended approach to fulfilling three of the seven V&V requirements (requirements 3.3.1.R, 3.3.2.R and 3.3.6.R).

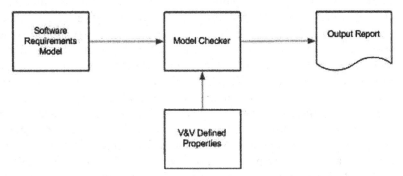

Fig. 3.15. Recommended approach to fulfilling V&V requirements 3.3.1.R,
3.3.2.R, and 3.3.6.R. The V&V team models the software requirements, they then
define properties that the system should display and they run these two through a
model checker to determine if the modeled software requirements actually display
the properties that the V&V team have defined.

The first task needed when taking this approach is that the V&V team
has to model the software requirements using the language of the model
checker. The abstraction techniques that most modeling languages provide
are an advantage to taking this approach. The disadvantage is that the analysts now have to learn not only the language of the model checker they
have to become familiar with the model checking process itself. However,
I believe that applying this effort up front will enable a more complete and
less complex V&V activity. The other disadvantage that you have to be
aware of is that once you have the software requirements modeled in the
appropriate language then you have to put in place a mechanism to maintain this model. Requirements change, as such your model will have to
change. The second task that V&V needs to perform is defining the properties that the software is expected to satisfy. So for example, if our system was responsible for monitoring and responding to excessive pressure
conditions and temperature conditions then the V&V analysts may define
the following property:

$$\forall t[\forall t', t - D \le t' \le t : \operatorname{Pr}essure(t') > Max\operatorname{Pr}essure \wedge Temperature(t') > MaxTemperature \rightarrow Danger(t)]$$

All this simply says is that for every instant t' in the interval [t-D,t], if
pressure is greater than the maximum pressure allowed and temperature
readings are greater than maximum temperature readings allowed then at
time t the system transitions into a danger state. In this instance, danger

initiates recovery measures. This is not verbatim from the book but I highly recommend reading the book Formal Methods for Real-Time Computing (Heitmeyer and Mandrioli 1996). My point in showing this example is that instead of the V&V analysts identifying requirements that they feel should exist they take a different approach and state the properties that the system shall exhibit. To me this capability is something that the development project does not and probably can not perform, given their budget and schedule constraints. The last task performed is to provide these items, the properties and the requirements model, as input to the model checker. The model checker determines whether or not the model satisfies the property. I seem to be a broken record but I have to say it again, it would be beneficial for V&V organizations to build repositories on things they care about. In the previous example, the V&V properties should be retained to be used again so that we don't always have to think up and write the properties that we care about.

A more static analysis approach is recommended for requirements 3.3.3.R and 3.3.4.R. For these two requirements the V&V team is concerned with assuring that the software requirements are completely defined and used consistently. There has been promising advancement in the area of static analysis and the use of tools to aid the domain expert in this assessment. One such area was in the tabular-based SCR method to specify requirements (Heitmeyer 1998). This type of method provides the capability to assure completeness and consistency with the requirements to some degree. The tabular-based method for specifying requirements may not be amenable to all types of requirements (e.g. memory scrubber) however it seems directly applicable to the control-type requirements that we are faced with in our critical applications (e.g. watchdog timer). One thing to note here is that in fulfilling the completeness requirements, the SCR approach focuses heavily on states and state transitions represented in the requirements. The same approach can then be integrated into the model checking discussed in Figure 3.15.

Static analysis approaches are recommended for meeting V&V requirement 3.3.5.R where the V&V team shall assure the software requirements comply with appropriate standards and engineering best practices. The reason that I suggest a static analysis approach is that tool support would greatly alleviate the burden on an analyst in checking requirements as to whether they follow a particular standard or best engineering practices. Tools that scan a requirements document and point out the inconsistencies between the identified standard and the document under evaluation should not be difficult at all to build. Key point though, they haven't been built and they should have. One of the problems though is what standard should be enforced? Well I would say we shouldn't identify one. The tool or tools should be configurable to the standard to which the project is using. So a configuration file would be needed to identify the standard to which the requirements document is compared against. There are other tools that also do automatic scanning that identify areas of the requirements that may or may not meet "best engineering practices". Things that these tools look for are the use of "TBDs" as well as an assortment of ambiguous terms. These types of tools greatly aid the analysts in meeting this one requirement.

The last requirement that needs to be met by the V&V team is requirement 3.3.7.R which provides assurance that all the requirements are testable. A static analysis approach is chosen to meet this requirement simply because there are tools that exist that automatically parse a requirements specification and generate test cases. The analyst could then take this set and identify which requirements that test cases could not be generated for. This tool support is concentrated on those requirements that are already defined in some tool (e.g. MATLAB). When you have requirements that are already defined in a particular language then you need to seek tools that support that language. For those requirements that are specified in a text document using the natural language then the task becomes a bit more manual. At a minimum, if you have to manually determine whether a requirement is testable run it against the following checklist. For the requirement under evaluation:

- Has it identified the state that the system is in?
- Has it identified the data that the requirement must act on?
- Has it clearly identified the action that the requirement is to perform?
- Has it identified the desired results of the action specified?
- Has it identified how other aspects of the system may be affected?

This is a very generic but solid checklist to use if you have to manually determine if a requirement is testable. I would suggest the following approach. For those software requirements that are within scope that have already been modeled in a specific language (i.e. you have fulfilled the first three V&V requirements by modeling the system and running the model through a model checker) then use tools that automatically generate test cases. For those software requirements that are not being modeled using a specific language then apply the basic checklist from above.

Figure 3.16 is a complete overview on how I would approach requirements analysis in order to fulfill the V&V requirements for this particular phase. You can see in the figure those circles with numbers in them. These circles are associated with a specific task that is fulfilling the particular requirement. This approach is something new and has only been

done minimally across projects. Formal methods are the buzz words that
are sometimes associated with this approach but I would suggest this is not
the case. It is more of a modeling and simulation approach that has its underlying theory being formal methods.

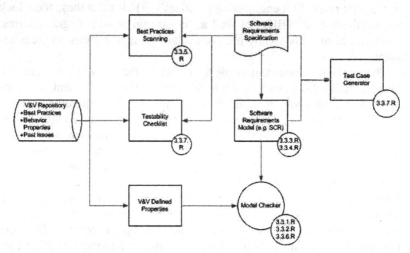

Fig. 3.16. Overview of requirements analysis tasks that fulfill the V&V requirements for the phase.

If you choose to employ this approach for requirements analysis then
there are three things you have to be aware of. First, it can become a configuration management nightmare if your models become very large and
the development project is constantly changing their requirements. This
can be a challenge because you have to ensure your models accurately reflect the software requirements. The second point is that if your modeling
discovers issues then you have to make sure it wasn't your models that
caused it. There is some additional effort needed to ensure that it wasn't
your model that caused the issue to surface. Lastly, there is going to be a
lot of effort spent up front in building the models as well as maintaining
them. I don't believe the data exists to show that it is well worth spending
the resources early on in the V&V project. All I can say is that from an
engineering perspective, this approach allows the V&V team to bring repeatable practices to the table that the development project will not plan to
do.

Section 3.3.2 Design Analysis

The design phase is the period in the development life-cycle where solutions to the software requirements are established. Designs as well as data constructs are established and linked to the specific software requirements in which they are the solution. Design is an iterative process through which requirements are translated into a 'blueprint' for constructing the system. Design begins with the requirements model to which it is transformed into 4-levels of design detail:

- The data structure
- The system architecture
- The interface representation
- The component level detail

Traditionally the data design transforms the information domain, from the requirements phase, into the data structures that will be required to implement the system. The inputs for the development team are the data dictionary and the Entity-Relationship (ER) diagrams. The architectural design defines the relationships between the major structural elements of the system. The input for doing this is usually the data flow diagrams (DFD). The interface design describes how the software communicates within itself, with other systems, and with users. The inputs to developing this are the DFDs, control specifications (CSpecs), and state transition diagrams (STD). Lastly, the component level design transforms structural elements of the architecture into a procedural description of the software components. The inputs to this are process specifications (PSpecs), STDs, and CSpecs.

It is during this time that the V&V team gets to assess the potential solution for the system. In the past, design analysis has been largely ad hoc. But I don't think that is mainly the fault of V&V, I also believe that software engineering is not as advanced in building designs or shall I say, documenting their designs. You may get certain scientific papers that describe the algorithms chosen for a particular design but I have not seen a complete software design for any project that I have ever been a part of. The V&V requirements for design analysis are presented in Table 3.13.

Table 3.13. V&V requirements that must be fulfilled during design analysis.

Requirement No.	V&V Requirement
3.3.1.D	V&V shall assure the right design elements have been identified.
3.3.2.D	V&V shall assure the design element satisfies the software re-

	quirements.
3.3.3.D	V&V shall assure the design elements are completely defined.
3.3.4.D	V&V shall assure that each design element is used consistently.
3.3.5.D	V&V shall assure the design element complies with appropriate standards and engineering practices.
3.3.6.D	V&V shall assure the logic and computational precision satisfy the needs of the system.
3.3.7.D	V&V shall assure all design elements are testable.

As stated before, the requirements presented in Table 3.13 are very similar to those presented during the requirements phase. Their only difference is the domain in which they operate. The requirements for requirements analysis focus on software requirements and system requirements. Those identified in Table 3.13 focus on software design elements and software requirements.

It is possible that the development group has used some design tool in order to architect a solution. This would have been revealed during the planning phase when input analysis was conducted. The analysis would have also determined whether or not the design tools had capabilities to perform the assessments that V&V needs to perform. Basically if the development team is using a tool to build the system then it probably has a modeling capability, this capability needs to be explored by the V&V team to determine if they can use it or they may need to translate the design into other formats.

So whichever format or method is chosen it must provide the capability to perform data flows, control flows, state transitions, and evaluations of algorithms. We are not done yet, it must also be able to present the behavior of the proposed solution as well as the timing attributes of its components. More than likely the V&V team will need to translate the developer's design into a format that provides the above capabilities. The same approach applies during design analysis as it did during requirements analysis. In figure 3.17 I present the approach for design analysis.

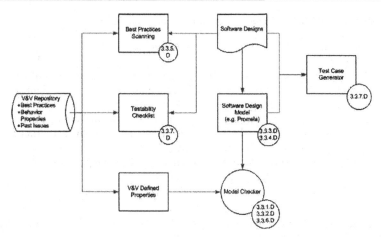

Fig. 3.17. Overview of design analysis tasks that fulfill the V&V requirements for design analysis.

So if sequence diagrams are used, state charts, or mealy machines, it does not matter. V&V has to put together an approach that fulfills the requirements presented in Table 3.13. A number of architecture description languages (ADLs) also exist for use by the V&V team. The majority provide mechanisms for describing the design components and the relationships with each other and the hardware being used in the system. The hardware being used has to be included in the assessments that V&V performs. In fulfilling their requirements V&V must take a systems approach towards assessing the design. This perspective is the first look at whether or not the proposed software solution can meet the needs of the system.

Section 3.3.3 Code Analysis

Code analysis is another bread and butter capability that V&V provides to the development project. The development project does not normally have the resources to explore all the potential problems that can be experienced during software execution. Also, small programming teams are normally employed that only focus on their area of development. During this time V&V is focused on determining how well the code conforms to the overall design specification and system requirements. Their objective is to determine the overall quality of the code. As such, V&V's requirements during code analysis are presented in Table 3.14.

Table 3.14. V&V requirements that must be fulfilled during code analysis.

Requirement No.	V&V Requirement
3.3.1.I	V&V shall assure the right code elements have been identified.
3.3.2.I	V&V shall assure the code element satisfies the design element.
3.3.3.I	V&V shall assure the code elements are completely defined.
3.3.4.I	V&V shall assure that each code element is used consistently.
3.3.5.I	V&V shall assure the code element complies with appropriate standards and engineering practices.
3.3.6.I	V&V shall assure the logic and computational precision satisfy the needs of the system.
3.3.7.I	V&V shall assure all code elements are testable.

I truly advocate the dynamic approaches that we have been discussing in the last two sections. However, I realize that there are a lot of organizations that take a manual approach to analyzing code. One step further is that some take a static analysis approach by scanning the code looking for common programming problems (i.e. variables are not initialized before they are used). I don't have a problem with these approaches but we have to take note that these approaches alone do not fulfill the requirements for V&V. Excuse my generics but there are a lot more things that V&V must do. Figure 3.18 is the recommended approach to fulfilling the code analysis requirements levied upon V&V.

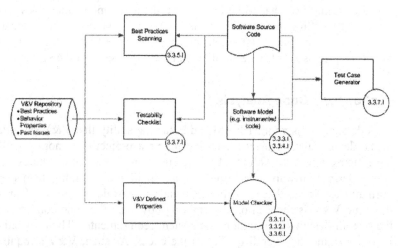

Fig. 3.18. Recommended approach to fulfilling the V&V requirements for code analysis.

The approach is quite similar to that taken for design analysis and requirements analysis. The V&V team takes the source code and models it. Modeling in this sense may not mean translating every line of code into another format. Simply instrumenting the code with assertions could be a model. Modeling the code using the language Promela is another model. The point is that some representation has to be developed so that its behavior can be assessed. Again, we are trying to fulfill the code analysis requirements which the first two are to assure the right software modules have been identified and that they satisfy the design modules. This involves answering the question is the function, *foo()*, the right function for the system. If so, does it satisfy the needs defined by *design module X?* The V&V analyst could use the design module to drive the development of assertions that check the input and output conditions. This can be considered a black box approach. Other assertions could be instrumented inside the code to validate the performance constraints identified by the design. If there are memory constraints identified by the system then the analysts can take the assembled code and parse it to identify all the pushes and pops to the stack to determine the amount of memory being used in specific instances of time. There are numerous methods that can be employed as well as tools to support them. The purpose of this section is to try and get across that dynamic analysis mixed with some static is the preferred approach.

The techniques that I want to discuss in this section are the ones that differ from the recommended approaches displayed in Figure 3.18. They don't totally differ from that approach but they are more manual in nature and require some discussion. The technique is software inspections. Inspections have been around since the 1970s and are still being used effectively. To put into a V&V perspective, inspections can fulfill all of the code analysis requirements but I would argue they can not fulfill them to the desired level of rigor. Inspections can also be used in the approach depicted in Figure 3.18 when fulfilling requirements 3.3.5.I and 3.3.7.I. These requirements deal with assuring the software complies with standards and best practices and assuring that the software is testable. Inspections can be quite useful in meeting these two requirements.

During a software inspection, small groups of analysts study work products independently and then meet to examine the work in detail. Work products are small, but complete, and analysts typically spend one to four hours reviewing the work product and related information before the inspection meeting. They were originally developed at IBM in the early 1970s (Fagan 1976). The traditional inspection process is comprised of the following steps:

- Planning – When a work product is complete, an inspection team is formed and a moderator is designated. The moderator ensures the work product satisfies the inspection entry criteria (i.e. code must be able to be compiled without error). Roles are assigned to the inspection team members, copies of the work product and related materials are distributed, and an examination meeting is scheduled.
- Overview – If inspectors are not familiar with the work product then an overview presentation is given by the author of the work product. Its purpose is to educate the inspectors and the moderator conducts it and the author presents the material.
- Preparation – Inspectors prepare individually for the examination meeting by thoroughly studying the work product and related materials. The objectives are to find as many defects as possible. There are various defect detection techniques that an inspector can employ, such as checklists.
- Examination – This is the meeting where the inspectors review the work product together. No time is spent discussing why defects occurred or how to correct them and only the work product is under scrutiny; criticism of the author must be avoided. All detected defects are classified and recorded. Examination is limited to a maximum of two hours. At the end of the meeting the team determines if the work product is acceptable as is, should be reworked with the moderator verifying the results, or reworked and then re-inspected.
- Rework – The author corrects all identified defects.
- Follow-up – The author's corrections are checked by the moderator. If the moderator is satisfied, the inspection is officially completed.

Since Fagan published his software inspection process, many organizations have experimented with, and modified, aspects of the process to fine-tune it to their environment. Others have modified changes to the approach (e.g. preparation step above) where instead of just finding defects the inspectors achieve an objective when reviewing the code (i.e. perspective based). I totally advocate this modification if your V&V group is going to use inspections or pseudo-inspections to fulfill the requirements of code analysis. The reason that I say this is that you will not achieve those requirements by simply conducting an inspection. For example, the second requirement that V&V must fulfill is assuring that the software satisfies the design. Conducting a code inspection to just look for defects does not satisfy this requirement. If you were to use a code inspection then two things would have to happen. First, the analysts would have to inspect the code with an objective of assuring the code satisfies the design. Second, the analysts would have to have some kind of tool support to fulfill the inspection. Inspections have traditionally been manually performed and to determine whether a module of code satisfies a particular design module is not easy to do manually.

Why did I spend so much time talking about inspections? If the V&V team elects to perform code analysis manually then they would be performing an inspection-like task. You can do this, although I don't advocate it given the technologies that exist today.

The other topic that I briefly mentioned above is tool support. When trying to find issues in the code as well as to assure the software complies with standards and engineering best practices there are an assortment of tools that exist that automatically checks the code. These tools help domain experts by flagging potential defects as well as aiding in the understanding of the code. Others methods that help out when taking the approach depicted in Figure 3.18 are assertion-based analysis which helps identify behaviors in the code to modeling in Promela and running the model through SPIN. The reason that I advocate the approach in Figure 3.18 is that the development projects can run their code through any available static analyzer. However, development is not going to analyze the code from a dynamic analysis perspective (e.g. software models represented in Promela and executed by SPIN). These activities not only fulfill the code analysis requirements they incorporate a different perspective that the developers will not have.

Section 3.3.4 Test Analysis

Test analysis is the time in which the V&V team determines whether or not the system is being tested adequately. Whether it is component testing, integration testing, system testing or acceptance testing that the V&V team is assessing, their objectives remain the same. Are they testing the system adequately? Now you are wondering what adequately means. The requirements that V&V must fulfill during test analysis are presented in Table 3.15. As usual you'll see that these requirements are very similar to all of the analyses that we have discussed. But again, their difference is that these requirements are focused on the test artifacts as well as the artifacts that they are testing.

Table 3.15. V&V requirements that must be fulfilled during test analysis.

Requirement No.	V&V Requirement
3.3.1.T	V&V shall assure the right test cases have been identified.
3.3.2.T	V&V shall assure the test case satisfies the unit under test.
3.3.3.T	V&V shall assure the test cases are completely defined.
3.3.4.T	V&V shall assure that each test case is used consistently.
3.3.5.T	V&V shall assure the test case complies with appropriate standards and engineering practices.
3.3.6.T	V&V shall assure the logic and computational precision satisfy the needs of the system.
3.3.7.T	V&V shall assure all test cases are testable.

Let's not get hung up on the terminology. If you don't call them test cases or if you call them test procedures then it doesn't really matter. The point is whatever you are using to exercise the system to show that the unit under test has been developed adequately then that is what V&V is concerned with.

The first two tasks that need to be performed are associated with requirements 3.3.1.T, 3.3.2.T, and 3.3.6.T. This is where the V&V analysts have to identify what test cases need to exist based on the unit under test. Figure 3.19 puts this into perspective.

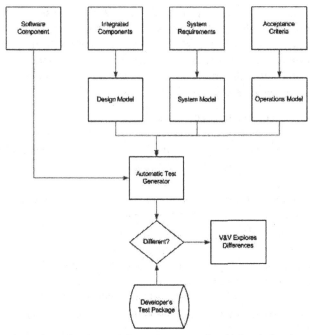

Fig. 3.19. Flow chart for determining what tests should be defined as well as whether the test adequately covers the unit under test.

As you can see in Figure 3.19 if the unit under test is a software component then the analysts need to identify the test that they feel should exist. So for example they may feel that every control branch in the software component should be exercised by the component tests. They would either manually develop the specific tests needed to do this or they would incorporate a tool. Actually, no way in this word they would do this step manually. Tools exist, so use them. This would be considered the test set that V&V recommends. They would then compare this set of tests with those engineered by the developers. Any inconsistencies would require exploration on the part of the domain expert and may result in V&V issues. This approach also covers the second V&V requirement in which V&V is to assure that the test adequately covers the unit under test. This basically means does the test exercise the component, integrated components, system needs, or operational needs adequately. If you can show that the test cases engineered by the developers are the same or refine those engineered by the V&V team then you can conclude that the test satisfies the unit under test. If not then V&V would author issues describing the shortfalls.

V&V requirement 3.3.3.T demands that V&V shall assure the test cases are completely defined. This could be performed manually by assessing each test case against a checklist. However, tools exist, not many at this point in time, to aid an analyst during this step. If you were to use a check-list then the following items need to appear in that checklist. At a minimum the test shall identify the following:

- The input required to execute the test
- The expect output of the test
- Any timing properties that need to be identified (i.e. especially if this is an integration test or system test)
- The objectives for the test
- The features of the system to be tested (i.e. provide links back to specific items (e.g. system requirements))
- The pass/fail criteria
- Environmental needs for executing the test
  - The necessary properties of the test environment
  - The physical characteristics of the test facilities
  - Additional tools needed during test execution
- How the measurements will be obtained and compared against pass/fail criteria

Successfully passing through the checklist will show that everything needed to be defined by the test is present. Again, this can be statically checked by tools and omissions can later be evaluated by V&V analysts.

V&V requirement 3.3.4.T provides assurance that each test is used con-sistently. What this means is that once the tests are established and shown to be complete they have to be used consistently every time. I have seen instances where the same test was run under certain environmental condi-tions (i.e. first with other components turned on) and then ran the second time with different environmental conditions (i.e. components turned off). They are using the same test but they are not using it consistently. Unfor-tunately I have only performed this step manually. I have not come across any systems tool that allowed an analyst to browse all the available tests.

The next requirement that needs to be met has again only been per-formed manually. V&V requirement 3.3.5.T provides assurance that the tests comply with standards and best practices. Could there be tool support in this area, of course. IEEE has for a long time documented the standard approaches to developing test documentation. Tools could be built that wrap around these standards to check for compliance. This step could also be coupled with those that fulfill requirement 3.3.3.T.

The last requirement that V&V must fulfill is V&V requirement 3.3.7.T which provides assurance that the tests themselves are testable. Say what? Well what this means is that the V&V analyst needs to answer the following three questions:

- Are the tests capable of simulating actual operating conditions?
- Are the fidelity of the models established and maintained?
- Is the test environment under configuration control?

The answers to these three questions will indicate whether or not the proposed tests can actually be executed to yield the desired results. If we are resting on the fact that if the software passes the proposed tests then we are a go for deployment then we need to understand the fidelity of the tests. Fulfilling this last requirement will do just that.

Before we leave the technical analysis sections I want to make sure the overall intent for these sections has been clearly communicated. In performing V&V we have four basic approaches; manual analysis, static analysis, dynamic analysis, and formal analysis. I am suggesting that the requirements for each phase have to be fulfilled regardless of the chosen approach. If manually reviewing the documentation is the chosen approach then the assessments have to take into consideration the V&V requirements and ensure all seven of the requirements have been met. If tools are selected then the V&V team has to ensure that the tools provide adequate coverage on the V&V requirements. The V&V phase is not complete until all requirements are met.

I am also suggesting that the V&V effort should take a more dynamic approach to executing their tasks. What this means is that analysts should reason more about the system's behavior during their analysis. Even if it is informal reasoning or using formal reasoning, the intent is for the analysts to derive sample executions of the system to determine whether the intended behavior has been captured. If the analysts go as far as developing models then these models even support the generation of test cases automatically, which fulfill another V&V requirement.

For those that were expecting a complete listing of available V&V tools then I apologize. By the time this gets printed there will be a new set of tools to select from. I will admit that a more in depth assessment needs to be conducted regarding all the methods available to V&V. This will be follow on work that would greatly benefit the evaluation and selection of V&V tools during project implementation. The overall intent for these sections was to clearly state exactly what it is that V&V achieves during their execution. I hope that this information alone will be valuable to the engineers and scientists in the trenches that are tasked with the job of making sure the system operates as expected.

Section 3.4. V&V Testing

Testing the system from a V&V perspective is really no different than the testing approaches used by the engineering community as a whole. The main difference lies in the objectives that testing is trying to achieve. For example, during development the developing organization will normally perform system testing in order to show that the system requirements have been met. On the other hand, the V&V team may perform system testing in order to break the system or understand where the system will break. These are two entirely different test strategies with only similarities in the way tests are developed.

Testing is the process of analyzing a software item to detect differences between existing and required conditions. It is also a valuable approach in evaluating the features of a system. It is an effective approach for probing for errors and weaknesses that reveal hidden faults. This is the greatest benefit that the V&V team can bring to the project during testing. The project is so focused on providing a useable system that sometimes their test strategies are only focused on showing that the system meets the user's needs. Where V&V is not concerned with delivering a system they are concerned with finding errors and weaknesses in the system.

This section is not a complete lesson on how to test software. It has been condensed to provide an overview since there is a wealth of information that exists in this domain. The intent of this overview is to put into perspective the few testing approaches that a V&V team may elect to take. A few examples are also given to improve on understanding. You can take this section as an overview to help guide you in establishing test plans and approaches.

Testing can be performed during each phase of the life cycle. During each phase, specific types of tests and their associated artifacts are developed. There are four types of tests that V&V can perform and they are described in Table 3.16.

Table 3.16. Different types of testing that can be performed by V&V.

Test Type	Test Description
Component	Conducted to verify the implementation of the design for one software element (e.g. unit, module).
Integration	Conducted to verify the integration of software elements until it

	results in a complete system.
System	Conducted to verify a completely integrated software system with its hardware components under simulated conditions.
Acceptance	Conducted to determine whether or not a system satisfies its acceptance criteria and to enable the customer to determine whether or not to accept the system.

These different types of tests are conducted at specific times during the life of the project. For example, component testing is conducted during the implementation phase. Integration, system, and acceptance testing is conducted during the test phase. Even though the execution of these tests occurs during those specific phases, there are additional tasks that V&V have to perform in order to prepare for testing. Test plans, test designs, test cases and test procedures all need to be developed. Developing these artifacts is performed throughout the life cycle, which is shown in Figure 3.20 and taken straight from IEEE standard 1059-1993.

V&V Task	Requirements	Design	Implementation	Test
Test Plan Generation	System Tests Acceptance Tests	Component Tests Integration Tests		
Test Design Generation		Component Tests Integration Tests System Tests Acceptance Tests		
Test Case Generation			Component Tests Integration Tests System Tests Acceptance Tests	
Test Procedure Generation			Component Tests Integration Tests System Tests	Acceptance Tests
Test Execution			Component Tests	Integration Tests System Tests Acceptance Tests

Fig. 3.20. V&V testing activities distributed across the life cycle. System test plans and acceptance test plans are developed during the requirements phase. Component test plans and integration test plans are developed during the design phase. Also during the design phase, test designs for all of the types of testing are developed.

As you can see in the figure, V&V testing activities are performed during specific phases of the life-cycle. System test plans and acceptance test plans are developed during the requirements phase. Component test plans and integration test plans are developed during the design phase. All test designs are generated during the design phase. All test cases are generated during the implementation phase. All test procedures, except for acceptance tests, are developed during the implementation phase. Also during the implementation phase the component tests are executed. The rest of the tests are executed during the test phase.

There are two approaches that can be taken to test a system, subsystem, or component and they are black box testing or white-box testing. Black box testing, or functional testing, is where tests are derived from the specification of the software. White box testing, or structural testing, is where tests are derived by considering the internal logic of the system. Black box testing is favored by the developers, since they focus mainly on showing that the specification has been met. V&V takes more of a white box testing approach because they are exploring the system's weaknesses in search of errors. It also seems logical that system tests and acceptance tests are more amenable to black box testing while component and integration testing seems to be associated more with white box testing. The rest of this section details the two approaches.

The astute reader is probably wondering about regression testing. Regression testing is performed normally after changes are made to the system or in addition to integration tests with the sole purpose of showing that that the original functionality has not been harmed with the preceding events. The reason that I have not included it in this discussion is that regression testing is more of a development activity and not normally performed by V&V. As such, I am hesitant to include it as one of the basic approaches for implementing V&V tasks.

Taking a black box approach to developing tests requires using the requirements documents and design documents. To proceed with a black box approach to testing requires seven generic tasks to be performed before any tests can be developed. The following list identifies these generic tasks to be taken for black-box testing:

- Study the requirements and identify each potential function.
- Identify any additional functions that may not have been documented.
- Identify the performance attributes or design constraints for the functions/components to be tested.
- Identify any operational procedures associated with the functions.
- Identify each state and each valid transition for the functions.
- Identify input and output data structures for the functions.
- Identify the arrival rates, formats, valid and invalid ranges for the functions.

Once this pre-work has been completed and the information generated then there are three basic ways that the V&V teams can use black box testing; equivalence partitioning, boundary value analysis, and cause and effect graphs.

Equivalence partitioning is based on the notion that specifications and designs sometime partition the set of all possible inputs and outputs into classes that receive equivalent treatment. These inputs and outputs result in two or more types of values, valid and invalid equivalence classes. So for example, the V&V analysts need to partition the program domain into a small number of equivalence classes and develop tests that provide coverage on each class. This is an inductive approach where conclusions about the entire input and output domain can be drawn from the behavior elicited by some representative members of it.

Boundary value analysis is a variant of equivalence partitioning and is based on the observation that software often fails at boundary values. As an example, functionality may indicate that temperature readings may range from -300 to +300 degrees Fahrenheit. Boundary value analysis would establish tests that not only include temperature readings of -300 and +300 but would also include values such as -301 and +302. The types of tests that are generated from this approach are those that explore the behavior of the system outside its design envelope. Rather than testing some random element from each equivalence class, boundary value analysis concentrates on the extreme values from each class

One weakness of the equivalence classes and boundary value analysis is that they do not test combinations of inputs and/or outputs. Cause and effect graphs are used to find those interesting combinations. Analysts can link input classes (cause) to output classes (effect) which will yield a directed graph. This graph is then used to develop tests.

White box testing focuses on testing the actual implementation, and the goal is to achieve full coverage of the component being tested. At this point in time the V&V team has to decide what coverage means to them. Coverage can be represented by number of statements, number of branches, or number of paths being visited during execution of the program. To aid the analysts in developing tests using a white box approach, a control flow graph (CFG) is essential. Nodes will denote actions (e.g. statements) and directed edges connect actions with subsequent actions in time. A path is a sequence of nodes connected through edges. Figure 3.21 is an example CFG for the following listing of code. The code is an implementation of the binary search algorithm.

```
int binSearch(float inArray[], float findMe, int size)
{
1) int left = 0;                      //Left side of the array
2) int right = size-1;                //Right side of the array
3) int arrayMiddle = 0;               //The middle of the array

   //Epsilon is the accuracy value: Since we are dealing with
   //real numbers comparisons on real numbers is risky (0.333 != (1/3))
   //So this solution, subtracts the values in the array from what you
   //are searching for, if the difference lies within epsilon, then they are
   //close enough and are considered equal.  (e.g. 3.14 = 3.14159)
4) float epsilon = 0.006;

   //The difference of the value in the array and
   //the value we are searching for.
5) float delta = 0.0;

   //Loop through the array until the left index has passed /the right index,
   //this means we have traversed the entire /array without finding the value.
6) while (right >= left)
   {
7)      arrayMiddle = (left+right)/2;
8)      delta = (findMe - inArray[arrayMiddle]);

        //If delta is negative then we know the value we are searching for is
        //less than the middle of the array. So shift the right index to the
        //(middle - 1) and convert delta to a positive number so that we can
        //test it against epsilon.
9)      if (delta < 0.0)
        {
10)             right = arrayMiddle - 1;
11)             delta = delta * -1.0;
        }
        else
        {
12)             left = arrayMiddle + 1;
        }
13)     if (delta <= epsilon)
        {
14)             return arrayMiddle;
        }
   }
15) return -1;
}
```

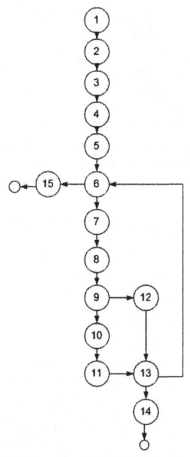

Fig. 3.21. Example Control Flow Graph (CFG) for the binary search algorithm. The numbers within the nodes represent the statement from the source code listing.

Control flow graphs can be very elaborate or very general. Tool support is very mature in this area and I advocate the use of a tool to support your testing activities.

If the V&V team wanted to focus their coverage on the source code statements and they wanted to test the component and achieve 100% statement coverage then that would require every statement in the program to be executed by the tests. Keep in mind that achieving full coverage of the statements does not ensure you have a correct program, it only means that every statement in the code will be executed. But having said that, anything less than this means that there is code that may be deployed that has not been exercised prior to operations. Using the graph in Figure 3.21 we have 5 paths through the graph.

- Path 1: 1-2-3-4-5-6-15
- Path 2: 1-2-3-4-5-6-7-8-9-10-11-13-14
- Path 3: 1-2-3-4-5-6-7-8-9-10-11-13-6
- Path 4: 1-2-3-4-5-6-7-8-9-12-13-14
- Path 5: 1-2-3-4-5-6-7-8-9-12-13-6

In order to provide full coverage of these paths then we would need to develop test data that ensures every path is taken. So for example, the 5 test cases in Table 3.17 could be used to exercise the 5 paths identified above.

Table 3.17. Example test data to exercise the paths through the code identified above.

Path	Value of inArray	Value of findMe	Value of size
One	{1.0, 2.0, 3.0, 4.0, 5.15, 6.14, 9.0}	2.0	0
Two	{1.0, 2.0, 3.0, 4.0, 5.15, 6.14, 9.0}	2.0	7
Three	{1.0, 2.0, 3.0, 4.0, 5.15, 6.14, 9.0}	2.9	7
Four	{1.0, 2.0, 3.0, 4.0, 5.15, 6.14, 9.0}	9.0	7
Five	{1.0, 2.0, 3.0, 4.0, 5.15, 6.14, 9.0}	8.0	7

However, you'll quickly see that you really don't need 5 individual test cases to exercise each path. One test case could be used to exercise all the paths. You'll also quickly realize that even though the test data chosen does exercise each of those paths, these particular examples don't provide a good coverage on the bounds of the array. However, you have achieved full statement coverage. This is a good example where a combination of black box and white box testing is beneficial. We can ensure that all statements are covered but we would incorporate boundary analysis to help identify the particular data to exercise the code (i.e. make the value you are searching for the first and last elements in the array, make sure epsilon is set to the right precision to guarantee accurate results).

Sometimes the V&V team may want to provide coverage, or combinations of, on the data being used in the code. These instances will arise when portions of the flow control is determined by the data rather than the code. The V&V team takes into consideration the definitions and uses of variables along the execution paths to help identify tests. A variable gets defined if it gets assigned a new value because of the execution of that statement. After that, the new value will be used in subsequent statements. Starting with the variable, graph (trace) through the code where it is used (referenced and defined). Using these graphs we can construct test to provide coverage for all the paths.

Even though I brushed over some of these approaches you have to understand that there are plenty of tools to support these approaches. Also, there are numerous approaches that can be incorporated based on the type of system you are assessing. For example, object oriented systems may drive the V&V team to test messages being passed between objects. However, some aspect of coverage always seems to be the underlying attribute. For the rest of this section I want to simply give a little more detail regarding the four test types and the documentation that needs to accompany the V&V test strategies.

Component testing is conducted to verify the implementation of the design for one software element (e.g. unit, module). Its purpose is to provide assurance that the program logic is complete, correct and works as designed. Component tests assess attributes of the software like timing constraints, memory constraints, performance at boundaries, interfaces, as well as under stress and error conditions. Component testing can be performed using a combination of black and white-box testing techniques but more white-box testing is employed during component testing.

Integration testing is a series of tests in which software components are combined and tested until the entire system has been integrated. The purpose is to provide assurance that the design objectives are met. The focus of integration testing is on the following:

- Compliance with the larger set of functional requirements at each stage of integration
- Correctness of subsystems and subsystem interfaces
- Assessment of timing and memory requirements as components are integrated
- Performance at boundaries and under stress conditions

Integration testing validates the structure of the design and how well the software components perform when they are integrated into the system structure. System testing then focuses on the integrated hardware and software system, usually under artificial conditions, to verify that the system meets its specified requirements.

The purpose of system testing is to provide assurance that the software, as a complete entity, complies with the system requirements. It focuses on the following:

- Compliance with all functional requirements as a complete software end item in the system environment
- Performance at hardware, software, user, and operator interfaces

- Performance at boundaries (e.g. data, interfaces)
- Performance under stress conditions

The primary goal is to validate that there are no defects among and omissions from the software and system requirements specification. Specific areas that may need to be tested are performance, security, reliability, and availability of the system.

Acceptance testing is often confused with system testing. It brings one additional focus to the testing regime. It can be considered as formal testing that is conducted to determine whether or not the system satisfies its acceptance criteria. It also enables the customer to determine whether or not to accept the system. The purpose is to provide assurance that customer's requirements and objectives are met and that all components are correctly included in a customer package. Acceptance testing focuses on the following:

- Compliance with acceptance requirements in an operational environment
- Compliance with installation procedures
- Compliance with user procedures

The Primary Goal is user validation and that the software complies with expectations, as reflected by the operational requirements. Users or representatives of the users need to be involved in establishing appropriate acceptance test plans. It is extremely beneficial to include them early on in the planning process so that the V&V team can understand what they feel the acceptance criteria are and plan as well as manage their expectations.

The documentation necessary to accompany the test types are test plans, test designs, test cases, test procedures, and test logs. Figure 3.22 shows a document hierarchy for the various test artifacts.

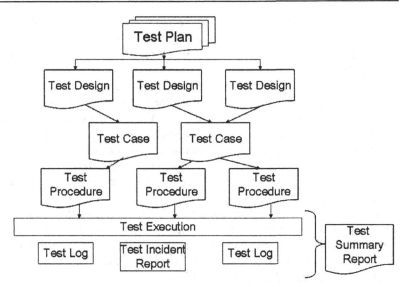

Fig. 3.22. Hierarchy of test documents that make up V&V testing.

These artifacts are further explained in the subsequent paragraphs. Test plans are developed for each level of testing. If you have separate plans for each level then develop an overarching V&V test plan that describes each level and how they are integrated together in order to represent the overall V&V test program. The areas to focus on when planning include:

- Transitioning from one phase or level to another
- Estimating the number of test cases and their duration
- Defining the test completion criteria
- Identifying areas of risk
- Allocating resources

For planning the V&V test strategy you need to identify the scope, approach, resources, and schedule of the testing activity. You also need to indicate what is to be tested, what is not to be tested, testing tasks to perform, people responsible, and the risks associated with testing. All of this will then be refined by the test designs. The purpose of the test design is to refine the approach laid out in the test plan. It needs to identify specific features to be tested by the design and it is used to associate the applicable test cases and test procedures that will be used to meet the design.

Test cases specify the actual input values and expected results. The goal in the generation of test cases is to exercise the logic and set up testing scenarios that will expose errors, omissions, and unexpected results. Keep in mind that one test case may be referenced by several test designs.

Lastly the test procedures specify all the steps required to operate the system and exercise the specified test cases in order to implement the associated test design. A combination of these artifacts is what is used to represent the V&V test strategy.

It would be an excellent discussion regarding whether or not all of these artifacts are actually needed. The reason for that statement is simply this. Testing can be a dynamic approach used by V&V to assess the system. If you were to compare testing with other analyses (e.g. traceability analysis – complete trace of requirements) you would wonder why they don't require an onslaught of documentation. The one main difference is that the V&V testing may be part of the development program and not just used as an approach to performing a V&V task. If it is part of the development project then it needs to be performed just as rigorously as the other engineering activities performed on the project. When used as an approach to perform a V&V task then I would understand if the V&V team chose not to produce formal documentation and relied on their engineering notebooks to document their approach and findings.

References

Fagan, M.E. (1976) Design and Code Inspections to Reduce Errors in Program Development, IBM Systems Journal., Vol. 15, No. 3

Heitmeyer, Constance, James Kirby Jr., Bruce Labaw, Myla Archer, Ramesh Bharadwaj (1998) Using Abstraction and Model Checking to Detect Safety Violations in Requirements Specifications, IEEE Transactions on Software Engineering, Volume 24, No. 11

Heitmeyer, Constance, Dino Mandrioli (1996) Formal Methods for Real-Time Computing, John Wiley & Sons Ltd., New York

Chapter 4: Systems V&V

Without a systems approach to performing verification and validation (V&V) all you can do is draw general conclusions about particular stages of a system's life. Not only are you constrained to individual phases of the life-cycle you can only verify that the software is an adequate representation of the documented behavior. There is another dimension that needs to be considered and that is validation. Is the right behavior evident in the system? This focal point looks beyond the software as well as the documented behavior and is often absent during development. The source code may be built adequately but if it doesn't operate as the user needs it to then what's the point in building the system? I am suggesting two things. First I believe that there is a correlation between each set of results that V&V produces during the different phases of the life-cycle. Second, to determine whether the software will meet the needs of the user and its intended application then V&V needs to take into consideration everything that can affect the software.

The intent of this chapter is to address where I believe V&V needs to be in the next decade. Specifically, we need to take a systems approach to performing V&V. Manually reviewing artifacts is an age old approach that we need to get away from. Domain experts are essential but we need to equip them with better tools and methods that will enable them to explore and reason about more complex and domain specific interactions the software has within itself and its surrounding environment. Manual techniques are limited to exploring that which is documented. The limits of human cognition make it difficult and possibly impossible to understand all the behaviors of the software.

There are two areas that I feel could be improved upon when performing V&V. The first area is related to the management practices and the second is related to the technical aspects of performing V&V. Management of V&V may even be considered ad hoc in some circumstances. Thankfully I have only been witness to one V&V project that didn't have management identified as a role on the team. The project felt that they just needed some assessments performed on specific artifacts (e.g. design module X). "We don't need a project manager, we need an analyst." That may have been the case and that may be acceptable but then again I wouldn't consider that to be V&V either.

The concept for including stakeholders is not new in the systems engineering world but it is fairly new to the V&V world. The health industry has taken advantage of this concept and I would like to see more V&V efforts follow suit. Including the stakeholders, at least during the planning phase, is essential. One of the things we have learned from systems engineering is that we need to manage the expectations of our stakeholders. V&V is no different and to do that we need to first understand what their expectations are. It is extremely difficult to be successful if you don't know what your stakeholders are expecting. You may get lucky but for the sake of this book let's just say luck won't be considered a viable management approach. Understanding and managing their expectations is much like requirements engineering. You need to elicit their needs and incorporate them into your solution. These needs can be a driver for the V&V objectives and V&V requirements, depending on your organizational model. Even if you are an independent V&V team, you must at least understand what your stakeholder's expectations are. The reason is that it provides you the insight into the system regarding what their concerns are and that will better enable you to identify what aspects of the system are error-prone.

Other systems engineering concepts that would greatly benefit V&V are the establishment of objectives and requirements. Objectives are the bedrock from which you focus your analyses. They also serve as an excellent communications tool. They state exactly what you are going to verify and validate with respect to the system software. They focus the V&V tasks by identifying which parts of the system are of concern. The entire software system does not need to be verified and validated. The V&V team is going to concentrate their efforts on those areas of the system that require additional assurance. As such, the objectives serve nicely in identifying the parts of the system V&V should focus on. A combination of the objectives and the V&V requirements identify what it is your team plans to achieve when you are done. Your team members as well as the stakeholders will know early on what to expect from V&V.

The idea of having a standard set of V&V requirements was pretty basic and straight forward. I felt that a common language was needed to bridge the gap between development and V&V. Engineers are well accustomed to defining requirements and developing solutions that meet the requirements. I don't believe that V&V should be any different. V&V should establish requirements that they are held to and design a solution that fulfills those requirements. To begin with I asserted there were fifteen standard requirements that V&V must fulfill every time (see Figure 4.1). These requirements are applicable to every V&V effort. My reasoning was based on the fact that in order to determine whether or not the software system was built adequately required the entire system to be assessed. This included the requirements, design, source code, and the tests. Only then could V&V judge the quality of the system. Just by looking at the requirements and the tests does not give ample insight into the design or the source code. The standard V&V requirements serve to establish a common framework from which we can institute a repeatable engineering activity of V&V.

Requirement No.	V&V Requirements
3.0	**Functional Requirements**
3.1	Traceability Analysis
3.1.1	V&V shall assure all the appropriate parent elements and child elements are in a relationship.
3.1.2	V&V shall assure that the parent elements are related to the right child elements.
3.1.3	V&V shall assure that relationships are consistent in their level of detail.
3.2	Interface Analysis
3.2.1	V&V shall assure that the right interface elements have been identified.
3.2.2	V&V shall assure all the interface elements are completely defined.
3.2.3	V&V shall assure that each interface element is used consistently.
3.2.4	V&V shall assure interface elements maintain the performance needs of the system.
3.2.5	V&V shall assure that interface elements are testable.
3.3	Technical Analysis
3.3.1	V&V shall assure the right child elements have been identified.
3.3.2	V&V shall assure the child element satisfies the parent element.
3.3.3	V&V shall assure the child elements are completely defined.
3.3.4	V&V shall assure that each child element is used consistently.
3.3.5	V&V shall assure the child element complies with appropriate standards and engineering practices.
3.3.6	V&V shall assure the logic and computational precision satisfy the needs of the system.
3.3.7	V&V shall assure all child elements are testable.

Fig. 4.1. Standard set of V&V requirements that must be fulfilled on every V&V effort. They are categorized as Traceability Analysis requirements, Interface Analysis requirements, and Technical Analysis requirements.

Figure 4.1 establishes the standard set of V&V requirements. They are requirements for traceability analysis, interface analysis, and technical analysis. This standard set of requirements are then refined based on the phase of the life-cycle. Figure 4.2 is an example of this refinement. As you can see in the figure, during the requirements phase the V&V team must fulfill traceability analysis requirements, interface analysis requirements, and requirements analysis requirements. The standard set or system-level V&V requirements, are simply qualified based on the phase in which you are in.

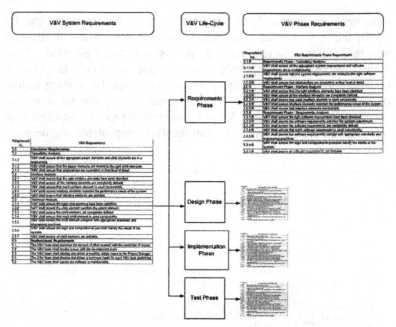

Fig. 4.2. Example refinement of the system-level V&V requirements for the requirements phase of the life-cycle. Each phase of the life-cycle will qualify the system-level requirements based on the artifacts that are applicable. So for example, during the implementation phase the V&V team will have the same set of requirements but they will be focusing on source code elements and design elements.

A V&V project must begin with these requirements and develop solutions that fulfill them. This serves as the common framework for which all V&V efforts shall operate. Tools, methods, and techniques are selected based on these requirements and is straight forward now that the criterion are established.

The remaining management approaches that I felt were new concepts and would yield great return dealt with controlling the project once it was being implemented. The first was instituting effectiveness measures. Effectiveness measures are used in the development community as indicators to the quality of the inspections being performed. They were successful then and I believe they can be successful now. The approach gives management insight into the adequacy of the issues discovered during analysis. This is achieved by categorizing the issues discovered by the V&V team. Again, these are indicators, not triggers. Just because certain things were found and others weren't does not mean that immediate action needs to be taken. It simply means that you need to understand why. Control gates were the other new idea that may be hard to digest at first. The thought was that control gates could be used to mitigate a lot of the risks associated with V&V. You would now have a review team looking at the potential problems the V&V team is going to be faced with instead of just one manager. Also, it institutes a level of rigor that I believe V&V needs to acquire. They need to be treated just like an engineering project which has to show that they are logically, not necessarily physically, ready to proceed to the next phase.

Technically I believe that a shift in the V&V paradigm is in order to not only provide validation of the software but to improve the approaches taken to verify the software. A shift from manual analysis to dynamic analysis would provide enormous benefit to the developing organization responsible for engineering the software. If V&V practiced manual analysis to fulfill their requirements then that would translate to bringing in domain experts to review the software artifacts. The development project has just as good people as the V&V team and they review the artifacts. So what makes the V&V personel a better choice to reviewing documents than the developers?

A shift in the paradigm would incorporate technical approaches that the developers aren't using (e.g. modeling the requirements). These approaches would clearly show that V&V is truly a complimentary activity and not repetitive. Modeling and simulation is something that the development team does not have the time or resources to do. You may argue that during testing they will incorporate these approaches but that is much too late in the software life-cycle. Using such a capability early on in the life-cycle will provide more stable requirements and lessen the risk of finding problems with requirements later on, which we know is quite costly.

Formal modeling and simulation bring a whole new perspective to analyzing artifacts. Instead of just reviewing artifacts and trying to comprehend all the possible behavioral patterns that the static documents portray, the analysts can model the information and execute it to extract the actual behavior. Instead of writing issues on a document, analysts will write issues about the behavior of the system. This alone is what is needed to make final conclusions regarding the system. Just because there are issues with documents does not mean that there are issues with the deployed system. A behavioral perspective would yield results that can be used to make more informed decisions regarding the deployment of a system. A generic representation for this approach is depicted in Figure 4.3.

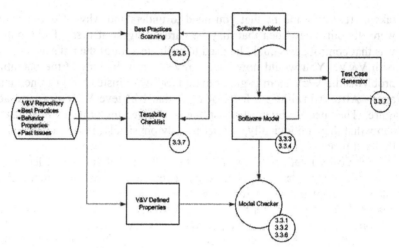

Fig. 4.3. A generic model for performing dynamic analysis during the software engineering life-cycle. During the requirements phase, the V&V team would take the software artifact, software requirements, and model it to prove certain properties or the omission of certain properties that V&V feel should exist. This model would then serve as a framework for other assessments to be performed (e.g. test case generation). The circles with numbers represent the V&V requirements in which the task fulfills.

The last significant discussion point tries to improve our current practices based on past results. Present and future V&V efforts MUST incorporate lessons learned from the past. We must learn from our past mistakes and incorporate them in our practices so that we don't repeat the mistakes of the past. This sounds simple enough, just build repositories of past software issues, best practices, and known accidents. It isn't that simple. Even though we have been diligent in documenting our known issues we haven't been good at integrating that knowledge into our engineering practices. I see this as something V&V could take the lead in for the software engineering community. Not only would V&V bring technical approaches not being used by the development community they would bring a well established knowledge base for best practices that support their conclusions.

I had mentioned in the beginning that a possible correlation existed between the V&V results from each of the life-cycle phases. These relationships could be the genesis for a series of assertions that could serve as best practices (i.e. using vague terms in the requirements creates ambiguity that is not testable). If we develop other assertions from our results then maybe there is an underlying theory that could explain them. We could use our fundamental theory, or theories, to explain why our assertions are true (or occasionally false). A much bigger leap is that our underlying theories could even generate many more assertions.

If I am a V&V analyst assessing the source code I will generate three sets of information. The first set of information encapsulates the understanding that I have gained from assessing the software. The second set of information may consist of issues that I write regarding the concerns that I have with the source code. The last set of information that I generate comes from fulfilling the V&V requirements for code analysis. Specifically I will know whether or not:

- The right source code elements have been defined.
- The source code elements satisfy the design.
- The source code elements are completely defined.
- The source code elements are consistently used.
- The source code elements comply with applicable standards and engineering best practices.
- The source code elements maintain the performance needs of the system.
- The source code elements are testable.

Now that I have these three sets of information how are they related to each other and with other sets of information learned from additional analyses (e.g. traceability analysis)? For example, if I know that the right source code elements have been defined but I have issues that show they can't be traced to any design element then what does that ultimately tell me? Could it be that the project will experience significant risk while maintaining the system? Are there other propositions that could be derived from the combination of this knowledge? There may be an underlying theory that when developed could explain such relationships. Maybe such a theory doesn't exist and our results for each phase are simply that, results for that phase.

I am not searching for a binary answer of yes or no regarding deployment. What I am seeking is an approach that integrates our results from each individual phase of the life-cycle. An approach that would yield propositions that can be easily translated into the development framework. I am searching for a unified theory for V&V. I envision a theory that integrates the general conclusions resulting from each of the life-cycle phases into a unified conclusion regarding the system as a whole. Maybe such a theory does not exist but I believe it demands exploration.

As a paradigm, V&V has been quite successful over the years. However, as our systems become more complex we can not rely on how we use to provide assurance. Our assessments have to employ technologies that will enable us to explore more in less time. It won't require a revolution but it will require change. Unfortunately change is difficult. It takes our engineers out of their comfort zone and puts them in a realm to which they are not normally found. As a leader you have to be willing to first accept these opportunities and second you have to be willing to lead from in front. That means you have to try these concepts out if you haven't already. For some of the readers these concepts are going to be regarded as "no brainers", simply because they are already practicing what I have discussed. For others they will be new concepts to which you should at least explore.

Whether you are an engineer, scientist, or manager you have to accept the responsibility to do everything that you possibly can to assure that you have a system worthy enough to deploy. I wish you well in your endeavors.

Appendix A

Throughout the book I have used project MUGSEY 0x01 as an example. This appendix provides all of the information that I have used regarding the project. The Multiple Gravitational Scientific Experiment Yield (MUGSEY) has the following program goals.

- To find the gravitational differences that the Earth influences on vehicles attempting to reach Low Earth Orbit (LEO)
- To provide cost effective launch and observatory platforms that can accommodate multiple scientific experiments that focus on studying the Earth's atmosphere, Earth's gravitational pull, and LEO.

The MUGSEY Program strives to provide a solution to meet these goals using common off the shelf technology. Examples may be model rockets and hot air balloons. To date, information suggests that neither of these technologies can put an observatory platform into LEO. Program MUGSEY shall achieve these goals using such technology. Indirect benefits of Program MUGSEY are:

- Independent parties can build scientific experiments that can piggy-back on MUGSEY,
- Missions within Program MUGSEY can be used in the classroom to teach software engineering and Verification and Validation (V&V) practices.

The first mission, MUGSEY 0x01, is the flagship mission that will prove the concept of launching and recovering a basic scientific platform. Even though the first mission is not planned to reach LEO, it focuses on first proving that off the shelf technology can provide the means to the end. The mission requirements for MUGSEY 0x01 are:

M1.0 MUGSEY 0x01 shall obtain an altitude of 50,000 feet.

Rationale: The first mission needs to show that it can achieve a suitable altitude while performing scientific experiments. Eventually higher altitudes will be achieved, but this first mission is to show that we can operate and recover a scientific platform in high altitude environments.

M2.0 MUGSEY 0x01 shall obtain pictures every 1,000 feet during ascent and descent.

Rationale: The first mission must show that it can operate a camera and take pictures during mission operations. Every 1,000 feet seems to be an adequate display of performance for the camera. Also, if a balloon is used then it will normally have an ascent rate of 1,000 feet per minute. So taking a picture every minute seems to be adequate to prove performance.

M3.0 MUGSEY 0x01 shall obtain temperature readings every 1,000 feet during ascent and descent.

Rationale: The first mission must show that it can operate temperature sensors during mission operations. Every 1,000 feet seems to be an adequate display of performance for the temperature sensors. Also, if a balloon is used then it will normally have an ascent rate of 1,000 feet per minute. So taking temperature readings every minute seems to be adequate to prove performance.

M4.0 MUGSEY 0x01 shall obtain altitude readings every 1,000 feet during ascent and descent.

Rationale: The first mission must show that it can operate an altimeter during mission operations. Every 1,000 feet seems to be an adequate display of performance for the altimeter. Also, if a balloon is used then it will normally have an ascent rate of 1,000 feet per minute. So taking altitude readings every minute seems to be adequate to prove performance.

M5.0 MUGSEY 0x01 shall obtain and telemeter position of the vehicle every 1,000 feet during ascent and descent.

Rationale: The first mission must show that it can operate a Global Positioning System (GPS) during mission operations. Every 1,000 feet seems to be an adequate display of performance for the GPS. Also, if a balloon is used then it will normally have an ascent rate of 1,000 feet per minute. So taking position readings every minute seems to be adequate to prove performance.

M6.0 MUGSEY 0x01 shall be recovered, in tact, so that all data can be down-linked and the vehicle configured to fly again within one week.

Rationale: The first mission must show that it can descend at an adequate rate so that it doesn't damage the package and all information can be retrieved from the computer. Also, damage must be minimal so that it can be reconfigured to fly again within a week.

The mission requirements, defined above, are further decomposed into system requirements. The system requirements are then decomposed into specific segments requirements. The segment requirements are then decomposed into specific element requirements. The element requirements are further decomposed into specific subsystem requirements. The following figure represents the concept for MUGSEY 0x01.

MUGSEY 0x01 System Concept

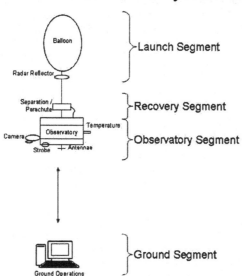

Fig. A.1. System concept for project MUGSEY 0x01.

Figure A.2 is the operational profile for the MUGSEY 0x01.

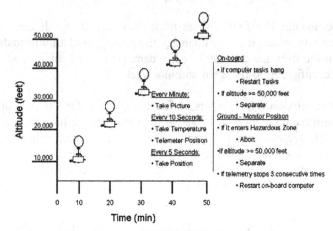

Fig. A.2. Operational profile for project MUGSEY 0x01.

Figure A.3 are the system requirements for project MUGSEY 0x01.

MUGSEY 0x01 System Requirements			
Number	Name	Description	Allocation
3.0	Functional Requirements	MUGSEY 0x01 shall obtain and store pictures, temperature readings, altitude readings, and position readings during ascent and descent.	N/A
3.1	Imaging	MUGSEY 0x01 shall acquire and store pictures during ascent and descent.	OS 2.2
3.1.1	Imaging Frequency	Pictures during ascent and descent shall be obtained at a rate of at least one picture every minute.	OS 2.2.3
3.1.2	Imaging Resolution	Pictures shall be of a resolution of 640 x 480.	OS 2.2.2
3.1.3	Imaging Stamp	Pictures shall be time-stamped with the local onboard time and position.	OS 2.2.4
3.1.4	Imaging Field of View	Pictures shall be taken at no more than 45 degrees nadir of MUGSEY 0x01	OS 2.2.1
3.2	Temperature	MUGSEY 0x01 shall obtain and store temperature readings during ascent and descent.	OS 2.3
3.2.1	Temperature Frequency	Temperature readings shall be taken at a frequency of at least once every 10 seconds.	OS 2.3.1
3.2.2	Temperature Resolution	Temperature readings shall be in Fahrenheit with a precision of two decimal places.	OS 2.3.2
3.2.3	Temperature Stamp	Temperature readings shall be time-stamped with the local onboard time and position.	OS 2.3.3
3.2.4	Temperature Field of View	Temperature readings shall be taken inside the observatory and outside the observatory.	OS 2.3.4
3.3	Position	MUGSEY 0x01 shall obtain and store position data during ascent and descent	OS 2.1
3.3.1	Position Data	MUGSEY 0x01 shall obtain and store altitude, longitude, and latitude readings during ascent and descent.	OS 2.1, OS 2.1.3
3.3.2	Position Data Frequency	Position readings shall be taken at a frequency of at least once per 5 seconds.	OS 2.1.1
3.3.3	Position Data Altitude Resolution	Altitude readings shall be taken in feet and with a precision of 2 decimal places.	OS 2.1.2, OS 2.1.4, OS 2.1.5
3.3.4	Position Data Position Resolution	Position readings shall be taken in degrees of longitude and latitude in this format (TBD) with a precision of 2 decimal places.	OS 2.1.2, OS 2.1.4
3.3.5	Position Data Altitude Stamp	Altitude readings shall be time-stamped with the local onboard time and position.	OS 2.1.5
3.3.6	Position Data Position Stamp	Position readings shall be time-stamped with local onboard time and altitude.	OS 2.1.3
3.4	Communication		
3.4.1	Telemetry	MUGSEY shall telemeter the position of the vehicle during ascent and descent to the ground segment.	OS 2.1.3, OS 2.4.3.1
3.4.2	Data Dump	MUGSEY 0x01 shall provide a connection to allow for data recovery.	OS 2.4.2.3
3.4.3	Commanding	MUGSEY 0x01 shall be able to receive and process commands	OS 2.4.6.2
3.4.3.1	Stored Commanding	MUGSEY 0x01 shall process a command sequence upon entering a failure scenario.	OS 2.4.5.1
3.4.3.2	Real Time Commanding	MUGSEY 0x01 shall receive commands from the ground and process them within 10 seconds.	OS 2.4.6.2
3.4.3.3	Invalidate Commands	MUGSEY 0x01 shall invalidate a command if it is not recognized.	OS 2.4.6.1
4.0	Recovery	MUGSEY 0x01 shall be recovered, in tact, so that all data can be downlinked and reconfigured to fly again within one week.	R3 3.0
4.1	Recovery Separation	MUGSEY 0x01 shall separate the observatory segment from the launch segment when commanded or when it reaches 30,000 feet in altitude.	OS 2.4.5.2, R3 3.2
4.1.1	Recovery Separation Performance	Separation shall occur within 5 seconds of initiation	R3 3.3
4.1.2	Recovery Separation Parachute	Upon separation, MUGSEY 0x01 shall deploy a parachute	R3 3.4
4.1.3	Recovery Separation Strobe	Upon separation, MUGSEY 0x01 shall turn on the strobe light.	R3 3.5
4.1.4	Recovery Separation Descent	MUGSEY 0x01 shall provide a descent rate of 5,000 ft/min.	R3 3.0
5.0	Operations	MUGSEY 0x01 provides a ground segment for operations during ascent and descent.	Ground
5.1	Receive Telemetry	MUGSEY 0x01 shall be able to receive all telemetry during ascent and descent.	Ground
5.2	Commanding	MUGSEY 0x01 operations shall send commands during ascent and descent from the ground operations.	Ground
6.0	Nonfunctional Requirements	MUGSEY 0x01 shall comply with all the requirements within this section	N/A
6.1	Ascent	MUGSEY 0x01 shall achieve an altitude of 50,000 feet at a rate of 1,000 feet per minute.	LS 1.0
6.1.1	Altitude	MUGSEY 0x01 shall obtain an altitude of 50,000 feet	LS 1.1
6.1.2	Ascent Rate	MUGSEY 0x01 shall have an ascent rate of no more than 1000 feet per minute.	LS 1.4
6.2	FAA Compliance	MUGSEY 0x01 shall comply with all FAA regulations	N/A
6.2.1	Weight Compliance	MUGSEY 0x01 flight components shall not exceed a combined weight of 6 pounds.	LS 1.2
6.2.2	Mechanical Dimensions	MUGSEY 0x01 shall provide flight structures that do not exceed the following dimensions TBD	
6.2.3	Suspension	MUGSEY 0x01 shall require a force less than 50 pounds to allow for separation of the launching mechanism and the observatory mechanism.	LS 1.3
6.2.4	Radar Reflection	MUGSEY 0x01 shall reflect radar transmissions	LS 1.5
6.3	Fault Handling	MUGSEY 0x01 shall recognize when its subsystems are not responding and recover them within 5 minutes.	OS 2.1.6, OS 2.1.7
6.3.1	Science Faults	No failure in the system shall keep any of the science readings (images, temperature, altitude, and position) from being taken for no more than 5 minutes.	OS 2.4.2.1, OS 2.4.3
6.3.2	Abort Mission	MUGSEY 0x01 shall recognize when it enters a hazardous zone and abort the mission.	OS 2.4.5.1
6.4	Data Loss	All data shall be retrieved from MUGSEY 0x01 with no data loss.	OS 2.2.4.1, OS 2.4.3.3

Fig. A.3. System requirements for project MUGSEY 0x01

Figures A.4 – A.7 are the requirements for the observatory segment for project MUGSEY 0x01.

Observatory Segment	
Requirement ID	**Description**
OS 2.0	Observatory Segment consists of the Guidance Element, Imaging Element, Temperature Element, and Command and Data Handling (C&DH) Element.
OS 2.1	The Guidance Element obtains and stores altitude and position readings using a Global Positioning System (GPS) and the Memory Manager of the C&DH Element.
OS 2.1.1	The Guidance Element receives altitude and position data once every 5 seconds from GPS
OS 2.1.2	The Guidance Element shall interface with the GPS as defined in the GPS Interface Control Document.
OS 2.1.3	The Guidance Element shall packetize the altitude and position data along with the local time and send this packet to the Memory Manager and to the Telemetry Manager of the C&DH Element.
OS 2.1.4	Altitude and position readings shall be made and kept to a precision of 2 decimal places.
OS 2.1.5	Altitude readings shall be made and kept in units of feet.
OS 2.1.6	The Guidance Element shall update the Watchdog Timer matrix every 5 seconds when it successfully receives data from GPS.
OS 2.1.7	The Guidance Element shall invalidate the Watchdog Timer matrix if after 3 consecutive failures to read from GPS. It must make these consecutive readings within 15 seconds.
OS 2.1.8	Position readings shall be taken in degrees with longitude and latitude in this format (TBD) and kept to a precision of 2 decimal places.

Fig. A.4. Observatory Segment requirements for project MUGSEY 0x01.

Observatory Segment	
Requirement ID	**Description**
OS 2.2	The Imaging Element obtains and stores pictures during ascent and descent using a camera and the Memory Manager of the C&DH Element.
OS 2.2.1	The Imaging Element shall utilize a web camera that takes pictures no more than 45 degrees off nadir and has the following physical characteristics (TBD).
OS 2.2.2	The Imaging Element shall receive and maintain pictures from the web camera at a resolution of 640 x 480.
OS 2.2.3	The Imaging Element shall receive and maintain pictures from the web camera at least once per minute.
OS 2.2.4	The Imaging Element shall packetize all images and stamp with local onboard time, altitude, and position data.
OS 2.2.4.1	The Imaging Element shall use a lossless compression algorithm to packetize the data.
OS 2.2.5	The Imaging Element shall interface with the camera as defined by the camera Interface Control Document.
OS 2.2.6	The Imaging Element shall update the Watchdog Timer matrix every 5 seconds when it successfully receives data.
OS 2.2.7	The Imaging Element shall invalidate the Watchdog Timer matrix if after 3 consecutive failures to read from the web camera. It must make these consecutive readings within 15 seconds.

Fig. A.5. Observatory Segment requirements for project MUGSEY 0x01

Observatory Segment	
Requirement ID	**Description**
OS 2.3	The Temperature Element obtains and stores temperature readings during ascent and descent.
OS 2.3.1	The Temperature Element shall receive and maintain temperature readings from the temperature sensors at least once every 10 seconds.
OS 2.3.2	Temperature readings shall be made in units of Fahrenheit and maintained with a precision of 2 decimal places.
OS 2.3.3	Temperature readings shall be packeted with the local onboard time, position, and altitude.
OS 2.3.3.1	Temperature Element shall comply with the temperature Interface Control Document.
OS 2.3.4	Temperature sensors shall be located inside the observatory and outside the observatory.
OS 2.3.5	The Temperature Element shall update the Watchdog Timer matrix every 10 seconds when it successfully receives data.
OS 2.3.6	The Temperature Element shall invalidate the Watchdog Timer matrix if after 2 consecutive failures to read from either of the two temperature sensors.

Fig. A.6. Observatory Segment requirements for project MUGSEY 0x01.

Observatory Segment	
Requirement ID	**Description**
OS 2.4	Command and Data Handling Element
OS 2.4.1	Operating System
OS 2.4.1.1	The operating system shall provide the basic kernel, loading of software images, spawning of tasks, scheduling of tasks, and interfacing with other subsystems.
OS 2.4.2	Memory Manager
OS 2.4.2.1	Memory manager shall scrub memory and correct single bit upsets and detect multiple bit upsets.
OS 2.4.2.2	Memory manager shall scrub memory once every 5 seconds.
OS 2.4.2.3	Memory manager shall provide an interface to downlink the data after recovery.
OS 2.4.2.4	Memory manager shall provide storage of all data sent to it.
OS 2.4.3	Telemetry Manager
OS 2.4.3.1	Telemetry Manager shall send the position of the Observatory Element, to the ground, once every 10 seconds.
OS 2.4.3.2	Telemetry Manager shall provide an interface such that other subsystems can request altitude and position data.
OS 2.4.3.3	Telemetry Manager shall maintain the last valid packet of data from the Guidance subsystem
OS 2.4.4	Watchdog Timer
OS 2.4.4.1	The Watchdog Timer shall maintain a matrix of all tasks executing on the processor.
OS 2.4.4.2	The watchdog timer shall kill a software task and perform a warm restart if it detects that a task has not updated the matrix.
OS 2.4.4.3	The watchdog timer shall check the matrix every 15 seconds.
OS 2.4.5	Fault, Detection, Isolation, and Recovery (FDIR)
OS 2.4.5.1	If the observatory detects a descent rate of 5,000 feet per minute it shall dispatch a RECOVERY command sequence.
OS 2.4.5.2	If the observatory detects that it has achieved an altitude of 50,000 feet it shall issue a separate command to the Recovery Segment.
OS 2.4.6	Command Processing
OS 2.4.6.1	Command Processing shall validate all commands that are to be processed. If a command is not validated then it is discarded.
OS 2.4.6.2	Command Processing shall receive, depacket, and process real-time commands sent from the ground.
OS 2.4.6.3	Command Processing shall maintain a table of stored commands that can be issued via a mnemonic.
OS 2.4.7	Time Manager
OS 2.4.7.1	Time Manager shall maintain local on-board time and provide an interface for requesting subsystems.
OS 2.5	The Observatory Segment shall be able to sustain an impact of (TBD) lbs/sqr inch.

Fig. A.7. Observatory Segment requirements for project MUGSEY 0x01.

Figure A.8 is the breakdown of the design for project MUGSEY 0x01.

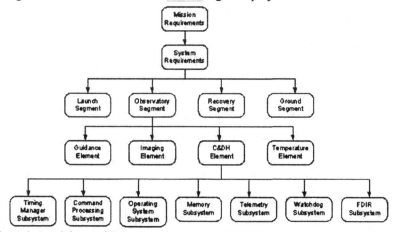

Fig. A.8. Breakdown of the system for project MUGSEY 0x01.

Index